WEST FRISIAN ISLANDS

THE DOLLART

W9-DFP-780

Dokkum

Emden

GRONINGEN

Franeker Leeuwarden   Groningen

LAUWERS

FRIESLAND

DRENTE

Medemblik

Enkhuizen
Hoorn

kmaar

ZUIDER

Koevorden

andam

ZEE   Kampen

sterdam

Zwolle   Vecht   BENTHEIM

OVERIJSSEL

OLLAND   GUELDERLAND

Deventer

TRECHT

Utrecht

Enschede

Ijssel

Wijk-bij-Duurstede

Zutphen

Arnhem

Tiel Neder Rijn

waal   Maas

Nijmegen

Kleve

Rhine

's Hertogenbosch

RABANT

ilburg

Geldern

Eindhoven

Venlo

N

GERMANY

Roermond

Meuse

LIMBURG

U M

Maastricht

Cologne

Tongres   Aachen

STEPHEN J.
VOORHIES

THE NETHERLANDS

IN

A CHANGING WORLD

THE NETHERLANDS
IN
A CHANGING WORLD

A Series of Essays

By

BART LANDHEER

ROY PUBLISHERS   *NEW YORK*

PRINTED IN THE UNITED STATES OF AMERICA
BY MARSTIN PRESS, INC., NEW YORK CITY
438

Preface

THIS book has been given the addition, "A Series of Essays," to its title as it does not intend to present a complete survey of Holland's present problems but merely a series of observations which the author made while abroad and certain reflections which years of occupation with these matters have given him. It does not present solutions or over-all philosophies or deep psychological analyses; it has been more its aim to show some of the changing facets of our problems. Some of these we have in common; some are our individual ones; none are really ever solved by writing about them but sometimes it may add to increasing awareness of what is wrong with ourselves and others; or if we consider nothing wrong with ourselves—and this has happened too—what trends we might expect in the future.

Our modern life seems very complicated at first, yet it is perhaps becoming simpler than life ever was before. We know so much of reality that we see no mysteries in ourselves or in others.

We are very certain of almost everything except what the other fellow will do next. Perhaps we should know better what we will do next ourselves and solve international and human problems that way.

If this volume serves a little to show that human problems are not so different anywhere, it has served its task.

It must be added that the opinions expressed in this book are those of the author as an individual and not in his capacity as a Netherlands Government Official.

November 12th, 1946

B. LANDHEER
New York, New York

Contents

CHAPTER I

Reflections On The Atlantic

AROUND THE MIDDLE of the Atlantic I began to get a certain feeling that Europe was somehow approaching and that I might gradually fall back into an attitude which belonged to bygone years. Perhaps it was in the mildness of the atmosphere—unusual for the North Atlantic around the middle of November—which reminded me of lazy afternoons spent upon Europe's white beaches; perhaps it was caused by the fact that the passengers were practically all European and that our conversation gravitated around the subjects which meant flesh and blood to all of us.

Having been absent from Holland for almost six years, it was natural that the picture of Holland as I knew it before the war was uppermost in my mind, obscured, to be sure, by the factual knowledge which I possessed of the changes which my native country had undergone. This saddening awareness of the destruction and suffering nevertheless did not entirely veil a strong nostalgia for Europe in whatever condition it might be.

The difference between Europe and the United States has been a subject of reflection for many generations of poets, philosophers and thinkers, a subject which forever acquires new and stimulating facets as it deals with a relationship between two factors which are themselves undergoing continuous change. And yet many of those who occupied themselves with this problem seem to feel that there are certain fundamental differences which will remain and cannot possibly be changed to any sizeable extent.

They point to the vast resources of the United States, the absence of national friction, the lack of stringent ideologies of long standing, and similar factors which we could not easily imagine to be of a temporary or unessential character.

Europe's overcrowdedness, its national intolerance, its inability to face problems on a practical level, its relative paucity in minerals are supposed to furnish the reverse side of the medal.

If these observations were conclusive, one could only agree with Goethe's words: "Happy art thou, America, with thine undreamt of riches."

Yet, there should be some reluctance in admitting that human happiness is determined to such an all-inclusive degree by materialistic considerations.

Is Europe but a relic of the past, to be admired for whatever is left of the treasures of bygone centuries, for its quaint atmosphere, its pleasant hotels and its attentive and well-mannered servants? Is that to be the future of the continent which was the cradle of the civilizations of the top nations of today while not even the remotest shores of the most obscure countries escaped its influence for better or for worse.

This was certainly not a question to which I could hope to gain an answer in a brief visit but there might be a possibility of getting an inkling of prevalent trends, of notions grown slowly which were observed long ago, of factors which the war had but expressed in a different way. The movements of our civilization are slow, and reflection might even be a better guide than observation—indeed an unorthodox thought for someone who intends to present his findings to the American people.

Or would it be better to see Europe only in the light of the statistics of destruction: of so many lives lost, so many destroyed by irreparable spiritual, moral or physical wounds, so many people displaced and homeless, so many factories and fields destroyed. Statistics are supposed to tell the truth, but what comfort can there be derived from these facts and figures

which omit the only really important factor, the human being and the elasticity of his mind.

Is not too much taken for granted in the American assumption of the common factors of human happiness: economic
stability, peace and freedom of expression, to express the
Four Freedoms in a slightly different way? The problems of
Europe, with its much greater differentiation, might prove
to require different methods to deal with them. It seems
somewhat over-optimistic to believe that the reconstruction
of Europe's economy would be synonymous with the creation
of a happy continent. Its problems go deeper and its spirit
cannot be expected to find an easy answer to the loss of its
position in the world.

If the philosophy of a nation is an indication of its present,
past and future, what philosophy could be found that would
answer its needs, what positive attitude could be expected in
a continent that has been crushed and defeated? Or, strangely
enough, would its salvation be found in its own outdated
philosophy of nationalism which can still distinguish between
the victors and the vanquished? The victors who most desperately try to believe in the resurrection of their former glory
tend to disregard the changed conditions of the world which
is witnessing the unheard of power of new super-nations.
And the vanquished are supposed to undergo the routine
punishment of the defeated in one of Europe's countless wars.

But behind all this, new and powerful forces are in motion
which aim to create a link—moral or legal—between the individual and a new world-organization-to-be. If these forces
are victorious, as we all hope, Europe will have to orient itself and cannot draw any further comfort from the more or
less glorious past of its sovereign nations. At the moment,
the fundamental requirements of such an attitude cannot be
but insufficiently realized in a continent which first has to
repair its loss of self-esteem and to regain a feeling of its own

national power and national virtue. There will be more than enough opportunity to quote instances of this.

It must be also acknowledged that the European nations— especially the smaller ones—have found little nourishment for any ideals they might have in the ways in which the great powers have gone about the creation of a new world organization. Too much idealism might be a dangerous thing but too little of it has a deadening effect on people who for years have suffered under a philosophy of stark realities, even if the realities were a case of mistaken identity. There is no doubt that the experiences of the past five years have introduced a strong element of skepticism in Europe, a skepticism which will not easily accept anything unless it has been clearly and definitely proved by facts to exist in reality and to hold some promise of permanence.

During the long and bitter years of occupation and starvation Europe's philosophers and thinkers had much opportunity to redream Thomas Moore's idea of a world state in all possible shapes and forms. Their theoretical discussions have so far received no hearing in the public forum of the world as we are now so convinced that law has to be based on power that we tend to forget that we are going to create a very static world if there is no distance foreseen between ideal and reality. The gradual approach between these two factors has so far constituted the progress of our world, and if there is not sufficient room between them, we might well ask ourselves whether we are not stultifying the growth of our human society. A living thing can either grow or die, but so far nothing has indicated that nature allows anything to be permanent.

In the eyes of many, we may be running the risk of sacrificing the happiness of the future to the security of the present. Why does the idea of equality lose in attractiveness if applied to states when it has been the motivating force within our society for a few centuries? Do we solve the problems of the state by transferring its very same qualities to larger units?

These questions are undoubtedly alive in the minds of those who through bitter suffering have once more created the dream of a better world.

In a recent book, "Nieuw Nederland" by the Dutch historian Jan Romein, the following passage occurs:

> "The collaboration between the three super-powers will not be guaranteed by anything after the war is over. It could break. It could also continue but be abused for a common suppression of the rest of the world or induce them through material distrust to divide the rest into their respective spheres of influence. In the first case everything, in the second almost everything would be lost. In a later phase the proposed federations* might not develop or conflicts might grow between them which would lead to a new war. In the first case everything would be undecided, in the second case decided but in both cases for the worse.
>
> "It might be that the new organization does not develop or only halfway. But it might also develop but become petrified. And even if this all should not happen, there is the danger of the increase in power of the national state. . . . Will there be enough elasticity after the war for thorough reforms when all suffering will again belong to the past?"

Thus we get a picture of a Europe which is eager to take a step forward but at the same time is distrustful of its own strength as well as of the larger nations which have now taken the lead in world affairs. Psychologically this is quite understandable. Europe itself has almost fallen back into a regional system which operates on even smaller units than the former national states, and the idea of larger federations of Europe as a whole or of sections of Europe has found no encouragement among the larger nations. We see more definitely a

---

* The author believes that there should be federations in Europe, Africa and Asia which would deal with the great powers on a basis of equality.

trend toward spheres of influence than any development toward a rational system of world organization which would envisage regions not too unequal in power.

On the other hand, it must be acknowledged that too great a departure from actual conditions would again create the same type of vague ideals which proved unsuccessful after the last war.

It is quite natural that the European nations feel that they should try to put their own house in order in the first place, and to hope for the best in regard to the world organization which is being built and which so far does not create any concrete picture in the minds of most people who realize vaguely that the influence of the small and medium nations is very insignificant indeed.

Yet, there is a certain danger in the idea of self-help and self-sufficiency. It will make the recovery of the various countries slower and have a tendency to loosen the ties which the economy of Western Europe had with the rest of the world. The choice lies, obviously, between a quicker recovery through huge foreign loans or a slower reconditioning of the economy which would make the repayment of foreign loans less of a burden but might entail the loss of markets which could not be re-won at a later date.

The author believes the first method to be preferable, but it is quite natural that for a creditor nation it would constitute quite a departure from long-established policy. It is, however, an outworn capitalist viewpoint to think that it is not quite "respectable" to borrow money, an idea which is deeply ingrained in the minds of some Dutch financiers.

If we are to avoid the errors of the past, the standard of living in various parts of the world should be equalized, up to a certain point, in order to avoid economic friction which would again lead to political conflicts. It would be a great danger to the peace of the world if Europe were to remain a low-standard-of-living area which would forever be a source of extreme political movements. If Europe were to unite on the basis of general dissatisfaction, it would be the worst powder keg the world has yet seen. The idea of dividing Europe into spheres of influence of the super-nations constitutes the first step on this dangerous road as it will be very tempting for the various European nations to play with a shift in their allegiance as a most useful political tool. It would also tend to create a deep cleavage inside the various countries—which has already become noticeable—between the forces of the right and those of the left, both influenced by factors which even make internal problems into facets of international power politics. Whether this will prove the basis of a harmonious development for nations whose economic problems are those of a declining prosperity is a matter about which one might well entertain grave doubts.

If the distinction between progressive and conservative forces were to become worldwide and make itself felt in international assemblies, we would reach a much more satisfactory stage than when this cleavage means a division along national lines. This division is of such artificiality that it cannot but create a warped and unnatural atmosphere in the international assemblies which should view the problems of the world with a matter-of-fact mentality.

World organization will need a world mentality in the same way as the national state created a national mentality. In this connection, it is interesting to record that the well-known liberal Dutch historian, Huizinga, devoted a study, after the last war, to the question of how the national characteristics of the Dutch mind could be defined. He arrived at the conclusion that the mentality of Holland's leading groups had become truly international and that it was virtually impossible to discover specific national traits in them. It is even more interesting to observe that this international mentality was by no means an indication of national weakness.

This is what Hitler assumed. He believed that the international mentality of the Dutch meant that the national spirit was lost. The bloody sacrifices of the five years' struggle for independence furnish proof of the error of Hitler's opinion. To be a good world citizen included being a good Dutchman in the same way that a good American can be a good Californian or New Yorker.

A higher stage in life doesn't exclude, but includes—as is clearly demonstrated by the whole growth of our civilization—the earlier stages. Hitler's conscious return to a lower stage was a sign of decadence as it meant the intentional abandonment of the effort to reach the next higher one.

It would be too much to expect that the average Dutchman, Belgian or Norwegian will develop too easily into a world citizen. This attitude will probably remain only realizable for relatively small groups in all countries. Every mental attitude needs an emotional foundation to become real and acquire enough strength to reach into the realm of action.

But there has definitely emerged a common attitude in certain parts of Europe which cannot but be strengthened by the disappointments and disillusionments of a post-war period. The average European today reads no more than a four-page newspaper which gives him only the bare essentials on world events. The foreign news is about the size of the summary on the front-page of the New York *Times*, and summaries seldom make encouraging or inspiring reading. They lack the background which gives perspective to mere facts and figures.

Thus, we can observe a sort of European attitude in the making. It is an attitude which cannot be easily defined. It definitely has a socialistic flavor but more in the spirit of social legislation and social provisions than in a spirit of dogmatic socialism. On the contrary, it is apt to stress the value of the individual, his rights and obligations, but viewed as a part of a faintly mystical whole. There is undoubtedly still a very strong influence of German thinking, and the new parties which are developing in various countries like to operate with terms as "the interest of the nation," "the well-being of the nation," etc., which mean a vague departure from the standard idea of the greatest happiness of the greatest number.

The appeal of the term "democracy" is not quite as magic as people in the United States like to think. Most Europeans would first ask for a definition which is always an embarrassing and difficult question to answer. Plato struggled with the problem that if we could define one concept correctly—for instance the fisherman, to use the classical example—we could then delimit all other concepts correctly through a process of elimination. But unfortunately, the possibility of a correct definition of anything is not logically possible as it presupposes a more complete knowledge than we actually possess.

However, it is not the place here to go into the philosophical possibility or non-possibility of a correct definition. Let us be satisfied to observe that the fact that so many Europeans have the courage to ask what "democracy" really means betrays a certain skepticism in regard to one of the white elephants of the modern world. Their skepticism probably also means that they do not quite believe either that "communism" is as black as it has lately been portrayed in several countries.

Let us consider what the term "democracy" might convey to a post-war European. A return to the world of 1939? The only Europeans interested in the world of 1939 are those who then were sitting at the top of a social pyramid whose shakiness they did not sufficiently realize. And this group consisted of a very small number of which the wiser undoubtedly realize the errors of the past.

It could hardly mean only political democracy as this has been put into effect quite completely in Western Europe since the last war. Nobody, for instance, in Holland wishes any change in the system of political democracy as far as the general application is concerned, although several political writers are urging a return to a direct tie between the voters and the respective candidates. There will be opportunity later to refer to the suggested changes in the electoral system.

An entirely different matter is the insufficient realization of social and economic democracy which was admitted and diagnosed as one of the shortcomings of the existing system. On these points we find general agreement on the desirability of these aims but little clarity on how they can be achieved.

"Social Democracy" is a rather vague term which would imply—at least to the author—a desire not to abuse, class differences as a means of hurting people's feelings in order to freeze the social system into a state of permanence which it would not possess on the basis of comparative achievement only. Whether this attitude—which is much more prevalent and more subtly put into effect in Europe than in the United States—can be changed is a psychological problem. It is strongly connected with social taboos, traditions, manners of speech and behavior and all other means whereby people consciously try to express that they belong to a certain group in our social system. If this behavior is organically connected with the function a person fulfills, it is a natural phenomenon. The matter becomes different when these attitudes are developed without a definite link with the work or function of the individual and become a purely defensive attitude which tries to conceal the non-existence or unessentiality of the function which it originally expressed.

A more static society develops such attitudes more strongly than a dynamic one where people are not supposed to stay in the same function for generations and where a desire for change is not so readily explained as a lack of character. To change this attitude in Europe it would be necessary to make its society more dynamic but we encounter the difficulty that a society which lives under the threat of decreasing prosperity has an added incentive to become static as an effort for change might easily lead to loss instead of gain.

The only way to effect a change would probably be through

the educational system which however also supports a caste-system instead of trying to break down some of the barriers. It is rather amazing that the educational reforms which are now under way in the Netherlands are opposed by the teachers who are out of sympathy with the idea that less learning but a more well-rounded education might make better citizens.

The general belief that the common suffering of the war would have lessened social distinctions was not confirmed too much by the experiences of the writer. He tends more to the belief that the war has brought about a shift in the class system but not a general desire to pay less attention to class differences. Perhaps, as someone has said jokingly, there are now 65 classes instead of 69 in the Netherlands, but this is about as far as the change goes.

It will be more interesting to record this shift in the layers of Dutch society than to attempt to prove that the entire system as such has become much simpler. The desire for such a change is undoubtedly present but there is the overwhelming difficulty that all good intentions submerge in a fear of adverse economic conditions. If this fear could be tempered, the psychological conditions for a change—or should we say "modernization"—are undoubtedly there although there is no reason to over-estimate the real significance of a certain equalization of manners among the various classes. This has the drawback which will be felt by admirers of the past of a loss in differentiation which is such a general attribute of modern life, however, that there is no reason to deplore its existence here. Since we live in the present age, we cannot but accept its limitations stoically and try to keep our belief that the advantages outweigh the disadvantages for mankind in its entirety, although there is no reason to deny that certain groups have every right to insist that past ages knew more about gracious living and intellectual achievement.

The crucial point around which the entire matter revolves is whether an increase in economic democracy could be achieved. This increase is a major point on the program of the leading political parties but we encounter again the same difficulty that, unless the national income as a whole could reach a higher level, shifts in its distribution could hardly have a very positive result.

In Europe itself the hopes of the people for speedy economic reconstruction are high, but one frequently finds a certain vagueness about the means whereby a permanent prosperity could be achieved. In the countries which were occupied, the world changes that took place are insufficiently realized and too many people aim at regaining the position which they held before the war. In some industrial circles there is great optimism about the future of Holland on the assumption that if an intelligent and industrious nation like the Dutch make the best of all new technical possibilities there is no reason for any gloomy opinion about the times to come.

Among more conservative businessmen and industrialists there is more concern about economic reconstruction. They feel that the strong tendency toward a semi-state socialism will put up more and more economic barriers which will make it difficult for Holland to regain its position as a commercial nation.

At the moment there is considerable grumbling about government red tape which has reached hitherto unheard of proportions. While people realize that a return to a free economy would be impossible at the moment, they feel that the interference with business goes further than necessary, and that the recovery could be quicker if the various economic controls were organized more efficiently.

The financial stability which Holland has achieved in a relatively short time is generally admired, but people are waiting impatiently for the removal or simplification of a number of control measures so that private initiative will have a larger field of operation.

Holland has traditionally been in favor of free trade, and many business people feel that as far as possible a gradual return to these principles should be put into effect. The term "regulated free economy" is heard frequently in the Netherlands nowadays, and this is generally considered to be the system toward which the western world is heading.

This makes any national planning difficult because it means that international economic agreements will determine to what extent there will be some freedom of movement for the national economies. Consequently, there is a certain haphazardness about the numerous plans which are in circulation at the moment as they are all based on ultimate factors which are as yet unknown and will probably remain unknown for a considerable period.

It is obvious that, operating with this vacuum, the inclination to plan on the basis of the past is being strengthened to a considerable extent.

Psychologically, this desire to return to the past will undoubtedly remain the strongest trait in the European psyche. The nations are not young enough in spirit to be very idealistic about the future, and, even if they were, reason does not seem to give a substantial basis for this idealism.

There may remain small groups who will be very actively interested in international arrangements but for the large masses there are signs of a lethargy which will not be overcome easily. At present this lethargy can be explained as an aftermath of the war, as a reaction to a period of anxiety and suspense. Fear has a strong hold over many people in Europe, and "Freedom from Fear" will not be achieved in a few years.

The feeling that disaster may come with every step, with every knock on the door, or even—too swift to notice—from the skies has faded, but not entirely. There still hangs a deep

gloom over Europe, the gloom of spiritual torture and uncertainty.

For the first time in centuries people have become close to
nature again. They know once more the deep-seated uncertainty of the primitive, the awareness of dangers which are
around them at all times and they also have the aversion to
words and phrases which have become hollow sounds to them.
Their confidence has to be regained, and they have to be re-
educated to the belief that human society can make a positive
contribution to their lives.

At the same time, people have become too passive, too
ready to ask and expect help from others. The feeling of
individual responsibility has been dulled in a period in which
the governmental powers were felt as a foreign hostile agency
with which no contact was possible.

Yet, however much we strain our belief in the social qualities of Man, we cannot get away from the fundamental fact
that the human being remains an individual who can be
actively interested only in those social groups which, in one
way or another, mean a positive contribution to his life.
With the return of life in Europe to a much more primitive
stage than before the war, people have become much more
selfish and disinterested in others than before. This attitude
cannot be remedied with words alone. The numerous relationships which our society involves have to be rebuilt slowly
and gradually. The too sudden attempts now to fill the
lacunae of the past five years have sometimes the aspects of
pathetic and amateurish attempts to rebuild at a moment's
notice matters which will require time, devotion and a certain amount of re-training and re-education.

A new stage in life may be reached through the attempts
to regain the old one; compromises will have to be made at
practically every point which will be different from the abstract planning which appeals to so many theoretical minds.
The cold facts of finance will put a brake on lofty schemes

for new cities to emerge from the present ruins. Sometimes it is as if the ruins of Europe had a frightening aspect of permanence about them.

Perhaps some of them should remain as permanent witnesses of the folly of war and destruction. They have become so characteristic of the European scene that they will not and cannot be easily forgotten. The cities of the past will assume legendary qualities and they may forever continue to surpass the structures of the future in the minds of those whose wounds have been too deep to heal again.

Or will the leveling-off process of modern civilization make it easy for people to forget? Perhaps it will prove that many institutions of the past which had outlived their usefulness have disappeared through the war not to be regretted by anybody.

The author found less evidence of a desire for renewal, however, than he expected. There is too strong a tendency to overlook reality and to give in to wishful thinking among many people. Many a good opportunity passes when those to whom it is offered do not understand that thousands or millions of people are waiting for similar opportunities, and that a lack of swiftness and eagerness is interpreted as a lack of interest.

The smaller nations of Western Europe are not yet accustomed to the enormous figures with which modern life operates. They magnify a thousandfold what is important to them and fail to see that the rest of the world is not particularly impressed or interested.

It is the tragedy of people who cannot understand the trends of the times.

There will, of course, be much improvement when relations with other countries become stronger and more frequent. The group which realizes that the world has changed—and which is so pitifully small now—will become larger and may guide the people toward the attitude which they will need to reach the place in the world they deserve.

The danger in a country like Holland lies perhaps not so much in the people. The large masses of the people, the farmers and workers, understand the fundamental problems of life better than most other people.

The danger comes more from the side of too many bosses, and half-bosses, the people who are important merely for their own protection. In periods of transition they are always the group which retards progress and makes it more costly and more difficult. In the years before the war they belonged to the "Hitler-is-not-so-bad group" which was found in all countries and which did as much for the rise of Hitlerism as Hitler himself. This group has come to life again and tries to maintain its position by yelling about the dangers of power-politics and by picturing differences between the big nations which are in reality much less then they pretend. They are afraid that the voice of the child might be heard saying, "But all the people on this earth could be happy so easily."

Let the smaller nations be the voice of the child in this world and let them continue to repeat that "all people on the earth could be happy so easily."

Perhaps then the many prejudices which are still in our way will disappear and we will be able to find simple solutions for simple things.

While the ship ploughed its way through a grey ocean—as ships have done for thousands of years—I could almost believe that we are only at the beginning of the history of mankind and that centuries of happiness are still in store for us if we can overcome the growing pains of the present period.

CHAPTER II

First Impressions

THE RESTLESSNESS among the passengers grew. Most of them had been absent from Holland for five and six years, and the anticipation was visible in their faces. They spoke little, as many of them must have been thinking of the friends and relatives who could not be there to meet them. The war had taken its toll from almost everybody.

"Where the white tops of the dunes glitter in the evening sun," somebody started to hum but gave it up after a few bars.

Finally a thin line appeared at the horizon, only it was not white on this greyish day, with a cold wind making the effort of staying on deck a patriotic one.

Most arrivals are somewhat anticlimactic as the emotion of returning generally precedes the actual event which thus remains slightly more than a visual experience.

The breakers leading to the harbor of the Hook of Holland looked slightly worse for wear and tear, and there was no lack of bunkers, destroyed houses and barbed wire in the part of the town that was visible. A few people pedaling around calmly on bicycles were the only sign of human life.

It stayed very much this way the twenty miles to Rotterdam. Partly ruined cities floated by, interspersed with stretches where there were few signs of destruction except the dismal sight of the destroyed wires of the railroad along the shores. But there was a strange comfort in the wide stretches of open land, beautiful in the subdued shade of green and with a *sub specie aeternitatis* aspect which only Europe can produce. It is as if the earth there breathes more slowly and rhythmically than in America, and the greater variety of colors in the landscape and the sky has a soothing effect on six years of repressed nostalgia.

Holland! There it was again in all its old beauty, as if it were above the wounds that wars can inflict and ready to resume its life of tilling the land and sailing the seas. Wondrous to be again on its winding rivers, older than any road man can build, and to see the cheerful houses which, in spite of the ruins among them, offered a spectacle of neatness and care.

Suddenly I felt reassured. The Holland I had known was still there. Its scars would heal, showing but faint traces as numerous other wars have left in Europe.

We were slowing down considerably. Soon the reason became obvious. Near Maassluis on the Waterway the Germans sank a number of ocean steamers in an effort to block the outlet to the sea. Two were sunk on the right shore (the "Zuiderdam" on September 22, 1944 and the "Dinteldyk" on the following day) and two on the left (the "Prince Willem V" on October 5, 1944 and the "Baud" on October 11, 1944). Only a small passage in the middle was left which was going to be closed by a ship that was held ready for this purpose in Rotterdam. Fortunately, the underground forces succeeded in sinking it in Rotterdam so that the Germans could not carry out their intentions. Thus, a small passage made the river navigable for ships up to 3000 tons. Immediately after the liberation the Dutch burned away segments of the sunken ships and were able to widen the passage so that the largest ocean steamers can reach Rotterdam again.

The half-submerged ships presented a sad spectacle, mute witnesses to the senselessness of war. But much more of this destruction became visible when we approached Rotterdam.

At first the shores near my birthplace still looked familiar, and the number of toppled-over cranes was smaller than I expected. Suddenly the link with the past broke off. When we rounded a corner, a large empty plain became visible where once the center of the city had been.

Rotterdam was no longer a town, it was more like a string of small provincial cities grouped around a sudden, unexpected desert.

This sensation became even stronger in the evening when a streetcar, rattling through a crowded street would suddenly enter this empty region where the life of the city came to an abrupt stop. Few people would venture to walk through this area at night, not because they feared any danger, but because they found it depressing to walk through the ghost-section of their formerly so active town.

There were a few centers of activity in the destroyed area of one and a half square miles. The townhall, post office, stock exchange, and a section of a large department store were still standing, and a lot of miniature shops in emergency buildings had sprung up around them. It was strange to see the names of fashionable old shops on little wooden shacks, with the same dignified face of the owner peering over the window sash. People in Holland don't change jobs much, and I was not amazed to find many people in the same offices or shops where they were six years ago. Generally they didn't look so very different either although some of them had thinned considerably. There was, perhaps, less cheerfulness than before, and expressions of tired indifference were rather frequent.

It struck me that a more martial spirit had taken possession of another part of the population. They were the former underground fighters who were now part of the army, police or the "Binnenlandsche Strydkrachten," the "Forces of the Interior" which were gradually being incorporated into the regular army.

There was a great variety of uniforms around, the new troops in their battle-outfits, the marines in American uniforms, the M.P. looking like Canadians, the old and proud state police, and occasionally some aged generals who would display their very outdated, but attractive, uniforms at their clubs. I was sure that there was as much diversity of opinion among them as of appearance, and I learned later that this assumption had not been erroneous.

It is one of the special qualities of Europe that life has so many more ties with the past than in the United States. Thus, a feeling of continuity is produced which has a soothing effect even in times of distress. It also causes a great love for forms which express these links with the past and which give contour to the lives of many who find the present a sad and discouraging spectacle. There are numerous possibilities to withdraw from life which do not exist on the other side of the Atlantic.

I had to think of this when we were rolling along the magnificent highway from Rotterdam to the Hague, with the graceful spires of Delft rising to the left as the flow of modern traffic detours this quaint and ancient city. The number of cars on the roads astonished me, and I was told later that the traffic amounts to about 75 percent of the pre-war volume.

People had apparently been very ingenious in hiding their cars, with haystacks having a high priority as the ideal cache. We were frequently stopped by young men with armbands and military bearing who seemed to disturb everybody's papers, as the general ambition was to be riding around in cars, and some people apparently thought that if it could not be done legally, then illegally would do. Whether a system of extensive controls really makes people law-abiding is a philosophical problem that we can come back to in a later chapter of this book.

So, there was Western Holland again, much as it had been before the war but somewhat pathetic and disorganized. I had always resented the urbanization of this part of Holland where one town practically ran into the other, and only small stretches of pastureland interrupted the reappearance of neat rows of infinitely dull brick houses, one after the other as if this eternal repetition of things not noticeable for their qualities would become more important by producing them in quantity.

Western Holland had always given me the feeling that the good earth was too far away or too systematically arranged to have any deeper appeal any longer. Somehow the horizons seemed somewhat wider this time, perhaps because I became used to creeping through depressingly diabolic tunnels into the flatlands of New Jersey.

But such ideas are highly unorthodox when one returns to one's native land after six years of war. The spots of heroic battles should be properly recorded instead of giving in to individualistic complaints about the landscape. After all, who was I except a privileged traveller rolling along familiar roads in comfort and staring at the vast crowds of shabbily dressed people who mill around little shops looking at things which are not really for sale. Why was it their fate to be trampled under the feet of much bigger nations who already own so much more of the surface of the earth.

There was no answer from the crowds which went their way stoically enough and did not seem to mind too much the privations which they still had to suffer. How few needs people would really have if they were not forever urged to buy a lot of things they do not really want very badly. Who would not exchange an icebox or a radio for a little more freedom? But the machine of our modern economy moves on relentlessly until it will finally rob more and more people of the qualities we need most; wisdom, patience and kindness.

One small English car—English cars are preferred now in Holland because they use less gasoline—was approaching the Hague, the once dignified residence of the Queen, seat of the government and town of many wealthy people from the Indies. The English bombardment put a section of the city in ruins while the Germans had built their Atlantic Wall through some of the fairest sections.

The suburb of Voorburg still looked about the same and very much like most residential suburbs of most cities of the world. They always make you feel glad that you don't have to live there but otherwise they are really very pretty.

A few more streets which I didn't recognize because half of them had disappeared and consisted merely of orderly ruins, and there was the stately hotel where the government was putting up some of its more or less devoted servants. The air of dignity surrounded me with such swiftness that I almost lost my breath for a moment. But I quickly controlled myself and strode with appropriate bearing toward my room which was small, cosy and relatively warm. Having heard that things in Europe have a tendency to disappear, I locked all my closets which later proved to be an entirely unnecessary precaution in this graceful and charming old world hotel.

For more than two months I was going to have my meals there surrounded by cabinet members and other dignitaries. This threatened my digestion in the beginning but I soon noticed that the human being has a tendency to get used to almost anything. For the same period I trotted faithfully from government department to government department, trying to find out what made the clock really tick or why it didn't tick. Of course, so much government would have probably stifled me, were it not for visits to Rotterdam where a workman is still a workman and proud of it, to Amsterdam, the undamaged city of northern beauty, and to the other regions where the peacefulness of former days is intermingled with cruelly destroyed sections.

But for the moment I was settled in the cautious city of the government where people tread carefully so that they will not disturb the majesty which hangs over the beautiful buildings, serene ponds and luxurious houses. At least this was the impression I had before I could take a stroll through all sections of the city when I found that the Hague was showing plenty of war scars although there are many completely undamaged portions in the city. The first bad shock was provided by the famous Haagsche Bosch which was broken by the ugly concrete Atlantic Wall and in which only a few of the magnificent trees were still standing.

But already there were signs of reconstruction. A horse-drawn plough was slowly making its furrows across the stately lawn in the front of the park. It was a strange picture: on one side the ruins of the Bezuidenhout, on the other the canal with its undamaged patrician houses, in front of which there was a constant flow of traffic, and behind that the slow-moving horse with his master who seemed to have no other concern in the world but the reconstruction of his lawn. It was like a strangely twisted Vermeer, suddenly showing all the disharmony of one so-called civilization.

On a Saturday afternoon I decided that I would walk to Scheveningen, the famous beach resort of the Hague. There were few pedestrians although the streetcars going in that direction were overflowing with people as all streetcars in the Netherlands nowadays are. I was therefore somewhat amazed when I was stopped at a bridge by a guard accompanied by a policeman who inquired where I was going. When I pointed out that this seemed an odd question as streetcars full of people were passing regularly, he stroked his chin and decided that there really was no objection to my having a stroll. After having offered him a cigarette to show that there were no hard feelings, I continued my solitary walk along the road where I had lived for a short time before the war.

There it was much the same as in most other places. The real atmosphere had not been spoiled. The beautifully built houses bordering the Westbroek-park were undamaged, but the houses on the other side looked as if a hurricane had hit them. They all can be repaired, however, but it was more serious that nothing much was left of the beautiful parks which surrounded Scheveningen. The line of dunes in the distance made up for much of the loss. One could write a novel about Holland's dunes, their weaving line along the white beaches, sometimes only one or two rows, sometimes stretching inland for seven or eight miles, with pine forests in hidden coves, full of the romantic appeal of a mountain landscape, with the murmured promise of the ocean in tangible vicinity. There is hardly a Dutchman without memories of hikes through this immensely charming scenery which does not seem to be repeated in other parts of the world. And just beyond the dunes, one comes upon the region of the tulips with their multi-colored patterns interwoven between pastures and canals and red-roofed villages. There is more charm and gaiety in these regions than almost anywhere else, whether the sun shines or the rain lashes down from the skies on the slow-drifting and imperturbable barges.

But these regions are really about 15 miles beyond Scheveningen, and thus, fortunately not too close to the Dutch "Atlantic City." Scheveningen's big hotels looked definitely more depressing than they do in normal times although their mixture of odd styles would make one wonder at all times what went on in the minds of those who built them. Watering places definitely do not belong to the twentieth century with their airs of a hospital for those who continuously overeat and have not learned to take proper care of the temple Gods which they hold on loan.

The famous boulevard along the ocean was still closed as German prisoners of war were busy getting the mines out. The Germans had done everything conceivable to destroy the beauty of Holland's coast. The beaches were full of stockades, barbed wire entanglements, bunkers, etc., while an atrocious tank-wall ran along the entire boulevard. It seems to be an engineering problem to get rid of these concrete walls as they cannot be blown up without endangering the nearby buildings. The problem will apparently be solved by having them topple over and disappear into the sand by their own weight.

The remainder of the "furor teutonicus" will be visible for a long time. To me, as a layman, there was little rhyme or reason apparent in some of the German fortifications, and sometimes I had the strong suspicion that some generals built fortifications in their sections without bothering too much about what the other fellow was doing. This may be malicious slander, because all armies, of course, are superbly organized and all led by very intelligent people.

Scheveningen, the Hague, ruins and riches, government buildings and just buildings, official talk and non-official talk, it all became somewhat tiresome after a while. I decided therefore that it had become high time to investigate some other parts of the country. Through the courteous assistance of the "Government Press Service," I obtained a small car with a chauffeur and a cheerful young man who could answer all questions I could possibly think of. I felt more thrilled about this trip than about getting aboard some transcontinental train or airliner. It was going to be a case of well-known regions revisited.

We took off with no more excitement than a smile on the face of the doorman. But excitement of a minor kind was due to come soon. We had gone hardly a few miles when the engine began to sputter angrily and then, with a sort of poisonous hiss of contempt, it stopped altogether.

"Cork," the chauffeur explained, "lots of cork in the gasoline now." He got out with the face of someone long accustomed to suffering, and blew through a piece of pipe. This seemed to do the trick, and we moved forward cheerfully again but for two and a half days he was going to repeat this performance every half hour or so, much to his disgust as it was bitterly cold and there was an un-Christian smile on the faces of passing drivers.

Going to Rotterdam did not excite us at all as we had seen it already, and our thirsty minds were merely interested in new things. The Maas Tunnel was something to marvel at, as modern and clean and shiny as the Lincoln Tunnel, and much more peaceful.

The story goes that the Germans intended to blow the tunnel up but that the underground bribed the officer in command of the area for half a million guilders. Truth or fiction? Nobody knows—or at least the author doesn't—but, at any rate it is good of the tunnel still to be there.

More modern roads, more factories, more pastures and more towns. Then we came to a part of the country which looks much more deserted, the region between the great rivers Maas and Waal which together carry the water-volume of the Rhine, not counting a few additional raindrops.

This is the part of the country where the rushes and reeds come from that are used for dike-building all over Holland. Small villages are perched against the dikes. They breed a sturdy race of people who are famous as dike-builders all over the world. Hardinveld and Giessen are names with a good sound in Holland.

On this part of the trip, where there are rivers everywhere, we had an opportunity to admire the tremendous value which the Bailey bridges had for Holland. Without them it would have taken much longer to restore communications and starvation would have been far more widespread and of longer duration. We crossed Bailey bridges everywhere, across small canals or inlets, across creeks, across small rivers, and across large rivers.

The repair of bridges is in full swing, and most of the vital connections would be repaired after a fashion by the end of 1946. The two-and-a-half mile long bridge across the Moerdijk was already in use at the beginning of the year.

The reconstruction activities in Holland are truly amazing, and I found nothing but praise for the work that had been done in the first half year. In a later chapter what was achieved in this relatively brief period will be described.

It will always remain a source of astonishment how much difference there is in as small a country as Holland—about the size of Connecticut and Massachusetts combined—between the various provinces. We were now passing from the province of Utrecht into North-Brabant and the change was immediately noticeable.

The intense green of the meadows seemed milder and interspersed with patches of pines and shrubs instead of the pensive willows. The houses were smaller and less austere, with a fondness for red shutters and a pleasant air of being places to live instead of a means to express one's philosopsy. Brabant is the country of Breugel and Rubens, of a pagan lust for living although it is in the almost exclusively Roman Catholic part of Holland. Churches and convents are strewn all over the countryside, and there is the pleasant aspect of the good pastor in the vineyard. But it has not been the part where industry and commerce thrived first. It remained rural and had a lower standard of living until several large industries developed in Brabant in the last decades.

Philips' Electrical Industries and Bata changed the face—and in some respects, also, the peace—of Brabant, and today one can drive through a small hamlet that has changed little in the past centuries and see hugh modern factories belching smoke in the distance. Islands of American efficiency arise in an ocean of peaceful and leisurely casualness. The casual people resent the efficient ones whom they suspect of being less human, less amiable and somewhat colorless, with no real understanding for the good things of the earth. The "carriers of modern civilization," on the other hand, regard their rural neighbors as somewhat backward, and they go around splitting atoms and inventing as if they were really certain that these things are going to make people happier than they were in the past.

The author belongs more to the school of casualists and generally cannot refrain from heaving a sigh of relief when he escapes from the modern temples of industry and commerce, but due to the process of long and careful training he is still willing to admit that they are the necessary foundation of modern life. But let us get busy and build a superstructure on our economic foundation of freedom, grace and art, instead of forever talking about problems and solutions. Freedom is ours if we can only see it and if we could cool our muddled brains with contemplation which is so vastly superior to action without purpose. Praise to the man who does not always pretend to be so frightfully busy!

Night was descending, and our interest in general affairs was replaced by a more direct interest in food and lodgings. The world seemed to have changed little when we finally wound up in the parlor of a hotel in a small city where the local dignitaries gathered for the evening. They were carefully separated according to their rank in the local hierarchy, and conversation was conducted in whispers. This, at any rate, was very soothing.

For the next day a visit to the island of Walcheren was on the schedule. Once it had been one of the most colorful and attractive spots on the earth, now it is called "heartbreak island."

When the city of Antwerp had been freed, it became necessary for the Allies to gain mastery over the Scheldt River which leads to the port. The Germans were still holding Walcheren Island which dominates the entrance to the river. Through repeated bombings in the period of 1944, the British succeeded in breaching the dike in four different places in order to flood the Germans out of their fortifications and to prepare the way for an invasion from the sea.

Contrary to a layman's belief, the flooding is not an easy matter. It depends on tides, winds, drainage and numerous other factors. When the first breach in the dike had been made, water was supposed to flow at the rate of 500 cubic meters per second during three hours of every day. The Dutch as well as the Germans had a plan to restrict the flooding: the Dutch by building dams around their villages; the Germans had the fantastic plan to build a six-mile dike across the island while the water was already flooding the country. In spite of the usual methods of labor conscription, manhunts, etc., the German plan hardly got started.

When British scout planes reconnoitered the island, they found that the flooding had been far less than anticipated. Three more times the Lancaster bombers roared over the island and breached the dike in three more places so that finally the water, rushing in from four different sides, reached the center of the island.

Day after day the water dug deeper channels into the fertile clay of the island, and many believed that one of Holland's most beautiful spots was forever lost. All efforts to save some of the villages or parts of the city of Middleburg were in vain. The rising water could not be checked.

To make the job complete, the locks at Flushing harbor were destroyed so that everywhere the seawater could enter freely. Walcheren had become once more a part of the ocean.

In the meantime embittered fighting was raging between the Germans and the Allies.

Life on Walcheren assumed nightmarish qualities. In Flushing the fight went on in Stalingrad fashion while on the remoter parts of the island people huddled together under almost Biblical conditions. Everything was heaped together on the few dry spots: people, animals, whatever people had been able to salvage. In this Noah's ark there was no need for rationing: chickens, cattle, pigs were there in quantities so that everybody just took what he needed. A few miles further on, in another village, there was nothing and people barely got enough to subsist. Ten or more different worlds on an area of a few square miles, with the droning of airplanes and the thunder of heavy artillery as the only thing which united them in this dismal expanse of grey and restless water.

Hours must have ticked by like years for those who could just wait and stare at the destruction of their homes and land. But, deeply religious, the people did not move and were determined to remain where they belonged.

Finally the stage was set for the last act.

On November 1, 1944, the British landed at various places on the coast of Walcheren, and, with heavy losses, fought their way inland. The battle of Walcheren was one of the most embittered of the war. On November 6 the Germans surrendered, not without a comic interlude. The German general was only willing to surrender to an Allied officer of equal rank. Hastily, a British major was promoted for ten minutes to a general, and Middleburg was free. In a few moments flags were out, people came running from their hiding places and a joyful crowd sang their national anthem openly and freely for the first time in almost six years.

As so often happened, the Germans surrendered rather easily in the end, and the majority seemed glad to be able to dispense with the heroic attitude.

Life readjusts itself quickly. When we drove through South Beveland, there was nothing but peace and quiet to observe. A war may scar a city badly but in the country there is always the feeling that the forces of nature are not disturbed too deeply by whatever Man does and that the earth hardly changes its appearance through all our feverish actions.

A farm here, a blot of houses in the distance, the neatly plowed fields and the white clouds sailing through the sky gave a feeling of permanence and tranquility.

But Walcheren would be different, a picture which we were almost afraid to face. Up to Middleburg things were still more or less normal although the fields to the left looked greyish and dismal.

There is a strange incongruity about war-ravaged areas that reminds one of early medieval pictures in which hell and heaven are intermingled in a seemingly illogical fashion. In the same way there are blocks of neat-looking houses interspersed with stretches of ruined ones in the destroyed cities of Europe. A kindly looking old lady may be seen reading a newspaper behind clean curtains with a wall of one brick-width dividing her from a scene of utter disorder and destruction. But, in one thing the Dutch are well ahead of other nations: their ruins look orderly and one would suspect them of a sneaking desire to plant flowers wherever their is a small patch of soil available.

In the abandoned bunkers and hideouts whole families were living who had put flowers in the tiny windows. Somehow there was an air of contentment although everything was extremely primitive and food was still barely sufficient. The Dutch have a sort of "never say die" mentality which has not been lost through the years of darkness and despair. They have a stoic quality which enables them to go about their task even under the most adverse conditions. They also have a great stubborness which makes them do things only if they want to and when they want to. The systematic Germans were often driven to despair over what they called Dutch stupidity.

The period of reconstruction is apt to bring out the best qualities of the Dutch. They are persistent, industrious, painstaking and amazingly patient from a New World point of view. With whatever equipment they have available, they are able to do a job which shows a great amount of skill and ingenuity.

They create the impression that reclaiming the land is a task they would even undertake with their own hands if there were no other tools available.

The image of post-war Holland which remains uppermost in my mind is the scenes of the dike repair on Walcheren, of the quiet movements of hundreds of men carrying heavy stones and placing them with great care in their proper places.

The small tug which took us around the last breach in the dike was subject to the strangest movements. Sometimes the water was hundreds of feet deep, sometimes we would run aground near miniature Niagara Falls of foaming water. It was hard to discover any system in the goings on: there were big floats in one spot, huge excavators in another, and then far out on the sea, a few ships would be dancing on the waves, waiting to bring in more floats that had to be sunk.

The whole scene reminded me of one of the final scenes in the second part of *Faust* when Faust gains deliverance through productive work.

"Nur wer strebend sich bemüht den kônnen wir erlösen."

If this continues to be Holland's device, there is no reason to worry about its future.

CHAPTER III

Psychological Reconstruction

WE HAVE NOT as yet learned to measure psychological reactions or found any methods to deal sensibly and scientifically with the problems of social groups. Nevertheless, the patterns of behavior are not overly complicated, if we attempt to visualize psychological processes from the outside. There is far too much use of slogans and phrases in cases which we could almost project on a screen. There is also too much generalization in the use of standard terms such as freedom, suppression, democracy, etc., which reverberate throughout the world every day without much thought being given to the weight they really carry.

If we look at any given society we always find a certain number of fundamental qualities which no amount of political, economic or social change can do away with.

In every society we find the three classes which are essential in making a go of the life of a group of human beings in their struggle against nature. Equality is a political concept which means that, at a given stage of development, a certain number of people protest an excessive amount of inequality. Complete equality in every sense would mean the end of any society as mankind would consist once more of self-sufficient, solitary individuals in the same way as in the beginning.

The existence of any society is based upon a division of functions which is reflected in a division into classes. It is hard to see that we could ever get away from a division into physical labor, the intermediary functions of clerical and executive work on a medium level, and the functions of a higher executive character and the professions insofar as they are

creative. These three groups have always existed in practically all forms of society since it passed its most primitive
stages, and there is every reason to assume that they will continue to exist in the future. This division into functions creates a difference in needs which has led to a differentiation in
income. It would be going much too far to say that the difference in incomes reflects with any accuracy the difference
in needs, because an element of power has always entered
into this part of our economic system. It could be argued,
however, that this condition is even observable in non-capi-
talistic societies although this is not the place to go into this
more deeply.

Society always has the form of a pyramid with all the possible variations which this form allows. The forms of pressure
within a given society are very limited in scope if we do not
look at the ideological weapons which are employed, but
only at possible forms of action.

A number of individuals in the lower strata will, by having
superior strength to the amount they really need, strive to
move upward. If the pressure from the upper layers is not
too great, a number of them will succeed in penetrating. If
the pressure of the upper layers—or perhaps we should say,
their weight—has become insufficient, whole groups of the
lower layers can move upward. This process would generally
be called "revolution" as the cohesion in the various layers
makes such a process more sudden than gradual although if
there is little cohesion in the various strata, it could undoubtedly also be gradual.

It is quite possible to find numerous examples of these various processes throughout history, but we shall limit ourselves here to some general observations as an introduction to
the subject of this chapter in the hope that it may aid to make
matters clearer.

Whatever changes occur within the pyramid do not alter
its fundamental qualities due to the very nature of its struc-

ture. Observed in this way, all social changes take on much simpler aspects than if we try to read them from the ideological presentations which are used to affect certain changes and which have the serious disadvantage—consciously or unconsciously—of influencing the observer, especially in our highly complicated modern world, so that he finally becomes an advocate of one of the numerous ideologies or merely adds another one instead of remaining the scientific observer who weighs and measures and then, in seclusion, draws certain conclusions from the material which he has gathered.

Another difficulty is that in our thinking we are always somewhat behind reality instead of, as a lot of cheerful optimists think, ahead of it. For the past sixty or seventy years we have continued to regard our social problems on a national basis while in reality much has occurred on an international level. However, this was either ignored or used in a devious manner, because it was felt that here was a territory where decency or honesty were not needed. The stabilization process which is brought about by law was in its initial stages, and, therefore, international relations were without a structure to give them permanence or stability.

This leads, of course, as one of many possible examples, to the conclusion that the comparison of our society with a pyramid is an over-simplification which we will maintain, however, in spite of its limited validity. The fact, however, that the law of the jungle still prevailed in international relations does not alter the fact that, as soon as they become stabilized, the social structure will, of necessity, also be comparable to a pyramid.

Before the war, as well as now, however, there were undoubtedly many social processes which we might term "subconscious" because, although they may be conscious in the minds of individuals, they are not conscious in the "social mind," or at least not officially admitted as being a part of it. Therefore, our pyramid, to return to this comparison, is partly submerged in a region of currents and counter-currents which are neither sufficiently known nor, as a consequence, sufficiently measured. We have in national as well as in international life the possibility of surprise, just as in our individual lives, because we do not probe sufficiently into this social subconscious, and have a tendency to think what we like to think or what we have been taught to think. The use of the social subconscious as a political means has been developed to a considerable extent by the Nazis who were quite right in their assumption that this would open up possibilities which remained closed to those who operated only in the conscious social realm. But they failed to understand that civilized society requires a number of taboos, and that their removal threatens the existence of society itself. The uprooting of social taboos very often only means their replacement by others, and in the case of Naziism even more new ones were created than existed before.

It would require a long and deep study to arrive at an opinion about what structural qualities our society needs to survive. If international society develops in such a way that it really merits this qualification, the structural requirements of national societies would naturally change. This would present many new problems because the structure of a world society would be totally different from a national one. The paramount qualities of a national society are all determined by the fact that many other similar societies exist. The possibility of conflict with these other societies causes all of the aspects which we generally attribute to the state: national territory, nationality and sovereignty. In the case of a world society, all these fundamental qualities would disappear and change into a picture of coordination and subordination instead of the un-coordinate existence of a number of entities of comparable weight and value. It is true enough that the urge of self-preservation puts certain checks on the behavior of individuals or individual nations, but this is the law of the jungle and not the previously agreed-to law of a civilized society.

For the moment, however, the possibilities of an organized world order are still remote as we are still in that stage which we described, where power determines the attitude of nations toward one another more than the concepts of law. We must not forget, however, that all historical growth of law has taken place in this same manner, namely on the basis of actually existing conditions. But we should also not forget that the social value of these laws was determined by the foresight and wisdom of their authors. If law merely freezes existing conditions, it lacks the elasticity which would give it a certain permanence. Therefore, the most lasting laws have been those which embody certain ideals like the American Constitution or the laws which developed during the time of the French Revolution. If the laws which determine the structure and status of a world organization do not have enough elasticity and do not embody the ideals of the group they embrace, they will not succeed in creating a smoothly functioning machinery. Of course, ideals which the entire world would have in common can only be of utter simplicity, but this would be their fundamental strength. The Atlantic Charter achieved the stating of these ideals in simple terms, but, unfortunately, the Atlantic Charter has lost its significance as a world document.

A law has validity only if it can be enforced, otherwise it becomes a moral precept. International laws, if they are to be enforced, have to establish a tie between the individual and a world organization. If a municipality, for instance, had the discretion to decide whether it wanted to prosecute a murderer or not, there would be no validity to our national laws.

In international life we can only visualize, at present, that the nations assume certain responsibilities in regard to their citizens, but the difficulty remains that the citizens can nowhere report any infringement upon their laws or rights. There would have to be a certain code of fundamental rights valid for everybody and a court to which violations could be reported in the same way as is done now in federal courts in the cases of violations of federal rights.

As long as such a condition cannot be reached, the national state remains the final agency with which the individual deals. A strange aspect of the state has always been that it exercises all rights, including those of life and death, over the individual while the individual may at all times have allegiance to organizations outside or beyond the state. In many cases this has led to compromises which are not always very logical and can create tragic conflicts. The state, in fact, has been a far more imperfect instrument of social life than is generally assumed, and it is sometimes hard to understand why so many people cling so tenaciously to so many of its institutions. The state as the organization of a social group has always been the subject of controversies concerning its aims, forms, functions, etc. This was partly because there were larger social organizations which developed different viewpoints about the function of the state and attempted to bring it back to a place which would make it subordinate to a larger organization.

With a world organization all these problems will become simpler because, in the first place, its functions will be more limited while, in the second place, the controversies about the form of modern life will have been whittled down to two major ones: the democratic capitalistic and the communistic socialistic one. Whether there is as much difference between these two as is generally claimed is doubtful because—*ceteris paribus*—they both approach state socialism in practice. The only difference is that in some countries the first system has remained state capitalistic while the other system is more state socialistic. Whether this difference really justifies a serious change should be answered in the negative from a theoretical point of view. A strange but perhaps somewhat precocious consideration is that if either of the two systems were to be applied to the entire world, it would be very hard to visualize what the essential difference would be.

It can only be repeated over and over again that modern life has become relatively simple. It rests upon the foundation of mass production which predetermines a number of its social problems. Under static conditions, mass production requires mass consumption which means that, generally speaking, the large number of producers, namely the workers, will also be the mass consumers. This means a higher economic level for the masses than in former ages, and consequently better education, a higher intellectual and social level, and, therefore, less difference between the executive class and the working class.

Comparing society again with a pyramid, this means that modern society has a broad basis which should give it considerable stability. If people could learn to think in terms of goods instead of in terms of money, they would realize that the major part of our production goes to the working classes. The fact that the masses are the main producers and the main consumers has also given them increased political weight under whatever system they may happen to live.

No ideology could ever develop which overlooked these fundamental facts. This gives a certain aspect of monotony to modern life which, ultimately, may become one of its major problems. Up to the present, the human being has never been able to lead a regulated, well-balanced life, but there is no reason to believe he should not enjoy it for 30, 300 or 3000 years as we may just be growing out of our adolescence.

A vague anticipation of the good life to come has permeated peoples and nations all over the world during the last twenty years. As a result nationalism was beginning to lose its appeal. The weakening of nationalism in the other countries at a time when no world organization had as yet developed to take over a number of the functions of the national state was a stronge temptation to Germany to make a last desperate gamble to become a world power—a gamble that came close to success in the beginning of the war.

Also, in National Socialism there was the latent idea of a world state—of course, in their case it would have been under the Teutonic master race—and this shows very clearly how strong the idea of a world state was even among the Germans who were politically and socially the most backward of Europe's nations.

The idea of the national state is still strong today in Europe where it originated; it has never played a dominant role in Asia, and the two leading countries of the world today, the United States and Russia, are not nationally minded in the same way as the European countries of the nineteenth century were. The equivalent of the idea of "Hispanidad" or of what "La France" means to a Frenchman cannot be easily found for an American or a Russian.

The conscious mind of a Western European is entirely filled with the national aspect of everything. The idea has penetrated him so completely that a Western European still thinks in a national way if he believes himself to be completely international and objective.

Both the United States and Russia have a world philosophy which they are convinced to be the best for the entire world, but this has not led to a nationalism in the old-fashioned sense of the word. Both systems developed as a reaction against the European upper class philosophy of the last few centuries, one more as a middle class revolution, the other as a revolution of the working class.

As both classes are essential to any given society, the fact that one system is slanted more toward the middle classes and the other toward the workers does not mean such a fundamental difference, since modern society has no choice about the weight which the working population carries as we tried to outline above. The economic function of a class in modern society determines it social and political function, at least on very broad lines.

In Western Europe revolutionary movements have left little of the aggressive spirit of nationalism, but international thinking runs purely along the lines of agreements among the states and shows little inclination toward larger units. Plans for a European federation or for smaller federations retain an academic flavor and find no support among the masses. European cultures are too much on a national basis to be able to blend and there is little likelihood that they ever will. Greater economic unity, on the other hand, seems to be in the making through bi-lateral or multi-lateral treaties. This greater economic cohesion will leave room only for the cultural aspects of the national spirit which should retain the diversity which was always one of Europe's major attractions.

Thus we see more markedly in the post-war period all trends which were in existence before the war. This should give us a clearer understanding of what went on during the war as well as of what may be expected in the future. We shall make an effort to exemplify this in the case of the Netherlands.

Prior to the war, the Netherlands was a well-balanced country of considerable wealth. Although it was politically a constitutional monarchy, it had many aspects of a plutocracy and an oligarchy. It had the admiration for wealth which is deeply rooted in human nature everywhere, but which had taken a special hold over the Western mind under the capitalistic system. Although capitalism originated from puritanism and had a strong element of restraint in it, it had gradually become the condition for a hedonistic society.

The name "capitalism" is frequently misunderstood and has really never been very clearly defined. It is mainly used to designate a society in which the state interferes little with the economic system and in which capital can be used to hire other people on a contract basis while nobody assumes very clear obligations toward the individual worker beyond the terms of this contract. Capitalism does not exist in this form any longer, but, while in some countries it was abolished radically, in other countries it has only been subject to restraining government measures ever since the turn of the century.

Holland was one of the countries in which restrictions had been placed upon capitalism. While as a system it was still in force, practically all the major political parties had been striving to put severe curbs on it.

One of the amazing characteristics of modern Holland is its very strong religiousness, combined with a talent for business. This combination of qualities is more pronounced in Holland than in other countries who found the roots of their modern development in Protestantism because it was stimulated by the geographic position of the country which made commerce, seafaring and agriculture its natural occupations.

This has given Holland a very strong practical sense which often has the appearance of phlegmatism. Yet, it cannot be said that the Dutch are not capable of strong emotions once they are thoroughly aroused as they proved in World War II as well as during the heroic struggle for independence in the seventeenth century. Their love for independence sometimes leads to unreasonable stubborness but from this stubborness heroism is born in times of duress.

Holland's heroes are fortunately individuals. As a nation it is far from militaristic and even rather undisciplined. It believes more in the pursuits of individuals and has neither a great talent for organization nor for coordination. These qualities are bred by necessity in larger countries, but in small ones everybody knows his neighbors too well to be very impressed by them.

The number of ties of a non-national character vastly surpassed those with a national imprint in pre-war Holland. The national cohesion was loose and the average Dutchman was either a philosopher who was concerned with his duties toward the supernatural or an internationalist with a humanistic flavor who thought of Europe as the seat of world culture. The idea of international collaboration was very strong in Holland after the turn of the century, and the idea of war was generally abhorred, feared or ignored as something that could never happen to Holland.

World events had their repercussions in Holland, but quieted down to normal proportions like the waves of the ocean breaking upon Holland's wide, placid beaches.

It is not too easy to determine exactly who belonged to the upper layer of the pyramid of Holland's society in pre-war days. There was no question of a simple distinction into the three major classes in the Netherlands at that time: it was such a complicated hierarchy that no one was ever quite sure about anybody's importance except his own.

The government officials, the nobility insofar as they also belonged to the owning classes or the government group, the patricians, the church leaders and the big business executives considered themselves as belonging to the top group. Scientists were held in high esteem inasmuch as they also held official positions as professors or otherwise. Free lance scientists, writers and artists were of a somewhat doubtful social category. If they were very outstanding or internationally known or possessed social position they could move on the fringes of the top layer.

Following the top group were those who had functions of less, but still considerable importance while those who had merely social position by virtue of title, family or rank belonged potentially to the upper group but had not activated this potentiality through any noticeable function.

The upper group was by no means closed, and a career based upon ability was entirely possible although it was naturally difficult in a country which was not very dynamic and progressed generally at a fairly even pace. Numerous examples of careers could be quoted, however, in politics, the professions and big business. In medium or small enterprises family management is very frequent in the Netherlands and extends even into various sections of big business.

Family ties in the Netherlands are very strong, and clannishness reaches rather deeply into its economic and social life. Consequently, a sort of patriarchal spirit is noticeable throughout all layers of Dutch life.

From these observations we can deduce what groups in the Netherlands were ill-adjusted to its social structure of pre-war days. They were, of course, the groups within which an outside enemy would look for support.

Politically two groups were opposed to the prevailing trend of regulated capitalism: the communists and the Nazis. In both cases these groups did not at first consist of persons who were completely convinced that something was radically wrong in the Netherlands, but of people who were dissastisfied with their status and who considered a different structure as the only way of escape. They were the people who did not have the power to move under the existing set-up and who, therefore, advocated a radical change.

The complaints of the Nazis met with little success in the Netherlands because their ideology was imported from another country, and contained very few points which applied to Dutch life.

One of the main tenets of Naziism, namely the so-called "decadence" of Western capitalism and the resultant need for a suppression of an excessively hedonistic attitude had but little validity for Dutch life which, on the whole, was wholesome and simple. Physically, the Dutch were considerably better specimens than their Eastern neighbors. The frantic cry about the downfall of Western civilization and the necessity of its reasserting itself by force was far-fetched to the ears of the Dutch who were more world conscious than the Germans and vaguely aware that a larger world was in the making in which Europe might play a smaller role than before, but which might still make it a highly esteemed member of the world family.

For these various reasons Naziism in the Netherlands was only attractive as a sort of conservative nationalistic party around which dissatisfied employers rallied who were afraid of the influence of labor, petty middle class people who believed that it would mean an increase in socialism, disgruntled intellectuals and those people who are always attracted by a new movement because they are in a permanently neurotic state. At no time was there a real leader of any significance among the Dutch Nazis.

The real weakness of Holland was the same as that of all Western countries, namely, the danger of unemployment and relative poverty in an otherwise prosperous community.

Economically there will always be a point at which the marginal worker is pushed out of production. Only social measures can solve this problem, but it would probably be considerably better if some kind of work would be created at all times for those who are no longer economically employable in order to prevent the creation of a dissatisfied group which has the tendency to become a political instrument.

Our civilization has shown little imagination in solving this problem. A combination of measures would probably be best, but there seems to be no more satisfactory solution than the undertaking of public works in times of depression. Certain public works should be set aside for this purpose, together with the funds to carry them out so that unemployment could always be broken after a certain time with periods of activity. Price subsidies are another possibility in order to keep essential products within the reach of the lowest income group. One of the main problems of our life remains the settling down to a more balanced period than we have ever known in the past. This involves certain psychological difficulties for those nations who have been taught for generations that history consists of a game of power politics among the nations, and have too many groups which live for the game of international politics.

The excitement which is caused by ever-recurring wars has become a psychological factor in the lives of many people who need considerable emotional readjustment to lead uneventful lives. The greater freedom of our moral thinking may prove a necessity to effect this change and then might gradually evolve into a code which would be radically different from the one which is now more or less "official" but which has little real foundation in life.

The impact of the German invasion upon the relatively normal and wholesome community of the Netherlands was tremendous. The actual invasion was short and left the people in a curious state—a combination of excitement and of being stunned by the swiftness of the blow. The top of the social pyramid had been removed and replaced by a foreign element which, in the beginning, was more seen than felt. The immediate result was that all latent feelings of dissatisfaction with the government came to the surface and led to the idea of having been left in the lurch or ill provided for, mingled with a feeling of despair about the future and a sort of attempt to make the best of things for the time being.

After reflection took the place of emotion, it did not take the people long to realize that, whatever mistakes might have been made in the past, the defeat would have been unavoidable in any case except through a world organization of which the Dutch had always been ardent but realistic advocates. At the same time, the harshness of the new alien order began gradually to be felt and to penetrate all layers of Dutch life. The resistance took on all aspects of the reaction of a sound organism against an outside force which tried to alter its structure. It comprised the entire population, but in strongly varying degrees with the exception of those groups which were unassimilated. Force was met with force whenever possible; the impact of German nationalism upon an internationally minded community created a Dutch nationalism which obviously sought its inspiration in those periods when Holland had been great in the world. The totalitarian methods of Germany-at-war caused a desire for an equally efficient machine and expressed itself in a criticism of the cumbersomeness of democratic methods. Insecurity, the wanton cruelty of the enemy and the breakdown of the economic system tended to aggravate these factors. Yet, the conviction remained among the large masses of the population that only utmost need justified this departure from the traditional standards. There was no attempt at any ideological justification. The physical suffering never really undermined the mental qualities of the people to a very deep degree, although it will take time to restore morale, initiative and reliability to their former status.

The forces which sprang up in Dutch life as a reaction against the Nazi occupation largely determine its present attitude. The national outlook is undoubtedly stronger than in pre-war days as is very evident, for instance, in the attitude regarding the Indies. The belief that the old democratic system was too cumbersome has led to a decrease in the number of parties and to an increase in weight of the executive branch of the government. The idea of an international organization still has a tremendous appeal for the Dutch, but they have very definitely decided to put their own house in order first, and they have attacked this task with all their available energy.

Undernourishment, isolation and forced inactivity over a prolonged period are the reasons that not all their efforts were equally well directed in the beginning, but it has not taken the Dutch long to regain their former stride.

Their psychological problem is, in the first place, to re-establish contact with the rest of the world and to get some idea of what their future place is going to be. A continued increase in population and the loss of economic relations with the rest of the world makes the long-term prospects for maintaining a high standard of living very difficult. This gives an element of insecurity to life which is felt very strongly by a race of people who are as conservative as the Dutch, and makes them try very hard to gain a favorable world which has some aspect of permanence. It also explains the strong interest in government positions which provide more security than private enterprise, although, ultimately, prosperity is determined by the amount of goods produced and not furthered by detours in production.

The exact amount of necessary and productive government control is one of the major problems of the world today. The poorer the conditions, the stronger the urge to have extensive controls which, on the other hand, often have a tendency to retard instead of aid recovery. To overcome this dilemma is the foremost problem of the countries that were occupied.

An estimate made for the national income for 1946 gives the high figure of about 8 billion guilders as compared with 5 billion before the war. If we take the higher prices into account—which stand at about 170 to 180 percent of the prewar level—we can conclude that production is somewhere around 70 or 80 percent of the pre-war level. This seems high, and one cannot quite deny that there still must be a certain amount of hidden inflation which is not immediately visible. Actual recovery is probably somewhat behind the figures given at present.

If we see the economic problems of Holland in terms of production of commodities, matters become much simpler. Before the war, Holland produced a certain quantity of goods, and in addition rendered a number of paid services in commerce to other countries and received returns on investments abroad. Of these three functions the first is undoubtedly capable of expansion as new inventions and production methods can be applied to increase production. This holds true even to a much greater degree for other countries so that total world production is going to be much beyond the pre-war level. The increased production will be taken up by home consumption and by exports.

The way we visualize the development of the world, exports in the long run should consist of those goods which other countries do not possess and should be on a basis of exchange and not of economic imperialism.

Although we are very far removed from this period, this may ultimately mean that the volume of world trade may be smaller than it will be in the intermediary stage. However, there is nothing frightening in this prospect as there is no reason to deplore an ultimate decline in trade, as long as the nations produce enough to satisfy their needs. Besides, total world consumption is still capable of such tremendous increase that trade among the nations may permanently remain on a high level. When we compute total world production against the world population, there is no reason for anything but a feeling of optimism if people can be taught to think in simple and direct terms about facts of world economy.

CHAPTER IV

Religion and Politics

WE HAVE HAD THE opportunity already to point out that the Dutch political parties are very insistent upon having complete ideologies which protect the human being from the cradle to the grave. Although, theoretically, the Netherlands fully recognizes the separation of church and state, there are few political parties which have ever paid more than lip service to this principle as they persistently bring their religious or philosophical thinking to bear on the problems of political life. This tendency, which is absent in the Anglo-Saxon countries, is hard to explain as it is a typical outcome of European psychology. European democracy has not been a conscious creation, except perhaps in the case of France, but the outcome of a long process of evolutions and revolutions. In each case, a group wanted to become the leading power in the state, and whenever it was not successful, it fell back to the rank of a political party.

Therefore, Europe's parties reflect her history and the changes in power which occurred, the rise and decline of ruling groups, instead of a steady march under a generally accepted constitution toward achievement of those aims which they consider best for the nation as a whole. We can understand this best by visualizing what would happen if a party were to gain the absolute majority. In most cases this would mean an immediate change of the constitution and an entire reorganization of the government and its functions. The European party system is a system of power politics which only survives because no party, fortunately, has ever gained an absolute majority. In fact, one has good reason to wonder which of the parties, if actually in power, would really maintain the existing constitution for any length of time. What would, for instance, a party do which advocates special schools for its adherents, if it were the party in control? Would it make the public schools conform to its own principles? The possibility of one party gaining control is never considered much in continental politics as the entire system is based upon the balance of power among various parties. The political system of Holland especially has always been characterized by multiplicity which, in 1934, led to the excessive number of 54 parties, later reduced by changes in the electoral laws to about 20.

This multiplicity is caused by the integration of ideological differences into Dutch life which cut vertically across the horizontal political groupings along economic and social lines that are found elsewhere. The four dominant ideologies are Protestantism, Catholicism, Liberalism and Socialism, all of which, however, have numerous variations and subdivisions. Of these four, Protestantism and Liberalism have the strongest roots in Dutch life and can be traced back to the origin of the Dutch state in the sixteenth century.

Before the war, there was hardly a section of Dutch life in which the division into four groups was not apparent. In labor unions, educational institutions, the youth movement, the radio societies, the press, etc., the same division was evident. The expectation that after the war there would be greater unity has not really materialized as we shall be able to point out later.

It remains a difficulty that of the four dominant ideologies, only Liberalism fully endorses the modern state while the other three would all shape the community according to their philosophy which means a stronger penetration of individual life than a government according to modern principles is entitled to get. The same trend of a greater penetration into individual life by the government is noticeable in all Western countries as a reaction against the liberal state of the

nineteenth and twentieth centuries which proved itself incapable of dealing with the excesses of capitalism. There is no
party nowadays in the Netherlands which does not advocate
extensive social measures, fair wage policies, etc., so that one
cannot escape the observation that such an extensive division
is somewhat academic in nature and leads to the formation
of political machines and power groups which form two
closely knit units within the state. For instance, population
policy is a matter which should be determined by the number
of people a country can reasonably be expected to support
and not by metaphysical principles. The interest of a community cannot be dealt with in a pre-determined way but
only in such a manner as actual conditions permit. Any
ideology is in reality a form of long term planning which
has the function of guiding a social group over a long period.
Today, however, our planning should be done on a world
basis and not on the foundation of any ideology which is
limited to certain groups or operates with principles which
are not subject to the consent of those governed.

The modern mind is not metaphysical and has, for the first
time in history, the opportunity to solve the problems of
economic and social life in a scientific way, that is strictly
on the basis of observed facts. It seems strange that a practical
country like Holland shows this penetration of its political
life by religious thinking and we can only understand this
as an ideological struggle which came out of a political conflict between opposing groups in the past. There is no logical
level on which these various ideologies can rest because the
differences in thinking can only be explained from political
and economic factors. It remains a struggle for power and
to see it as such might be a means of creating better understanding among the various groups.

During the war, there was a moment when it seemed that
greater political unity might be achieved. Shortly after the
invasions in May, 1940, representatives of the most important

political parties came together with the purpose of forming a political federation which was to issue a manifesto to the Netherlands people. Dr. Hendrik Colijn, the leader of the Anti-Revolutionary Party and former Prime Minister, had been requested to write this important document.

Representatives of the Roman Catholic, Anti-Revolutionary, Christian Historical, Social Democratic, Liberal and Liberal Democratic parties assembled to study this document. Colijn's statement emphasized that according to international law, a certain cooperation in daily matters with the occupying power was unavoidable but it also stated that no other future for the nation could be visualized except independence under the leadership of the House of Orange.

This phrasing of the principles of Dutch political life met with unanimous approval as it expressed clearly that there would be no compromise with the enemy.

The meeting was attended by two representatives of a group called the "Nederlandsche Gemeenschap" (Netherlands Commonwealth). Mr. G. Linthorst Homan, Queen's Commissioner in the Province of Groningen and I. E. de Quay, a professor at the Catholic Economic College of Tilburg in the Southern Netherlands. When Linthorst Homan handed the document to Seyss Inquart, the German Commissioner, he met with a negative attitude.

The Commissioner was not willing to concede the use of the phrase of "an independent Holland under leadership of the House of Orange." The representatives of the Anti-Revolutionary, Christian Historical and Liberal parties withdrew from the Netherlands Union as they were not interested in supporting a declaration which would omit the fundamental principles of their political thinking.

Nevertheless, Linthorst Homan, De Quay and a third non-politician, L. Einthoven, former Chief of Police of Rotterdam, decided to go ahead with the formation of the Netherlands Union as a counter weight against a possible increase in power of the National Socialist movement. The first proclamation of the Netherlands Union to the Netherlands people was issued on July 24, 1940. It stated:

"Out of the stress of our days a new duty is born, and we urge you to take up that task with us. We call upon you to strive with us for a new Netherlands unity, in accordance with our Netherlands character and through joint courageous labor. A first necessity to achieve this is the acknowledgement of a change in our relationships. National cooperation on the broadest basis must follow along with harmonious economic rehabilitation in which the entire labor section of our people is to cooperate. Social justice, too, would be a prerequisite so that young and old, strong and weak, will find work to do.

"These aims can be materialized," as is quoted in L. de Jong and Joseph W. F. Stoppleman's *The Lion Rampant,* New York, 1943, p.236, "only in our own Netherlands way, with full respect for our traditional spiritual liberty and tolerance.

"We are willing to do our work in cooperation with the Dutch authorities, and the occupying power. Netherlanders, give your utmost strength to our common cause. He who stands aside to 'wait and see' will only harm the good of our country. Join us now."

The program then outlined the main principles of the organization. It aimed at maintaining and strengthening the unity of the people in political, cultural and social economic fields. Economically, the Netherlands Union came out for "organic planning," a tenet which definitely betrayed an influence of National Socialist thinking. Politically, the Netherlands Union favored strong national unity, with a close relationship with the Netherlands East and West Indies.

Psychologically, the program of the Union consisted of a strange compromise: it stressed Dutch independence but was also willing to accept the reorganization of the world

on a basis which admitted many points of the "New Order."
It rallied the bewildered Dutch around the Dutch flag on
principles which were a Dutch version of wild nationalism
with a socialist flavor. It was no wonder that these principles,
which were the only possible ones under the existing circumstances, attracted many people and although the existing
political parties took a cool attitude toward the Netherlands
Union, membership rose in a short time to the amazing
figure of 800,000, about nine percent of the population.

It is not quite clear why the Germans supported the Union
in the beginning. They probably believed that it would be
a means of winning the Dutch over gradually to the New
Order, a task which would never have been achieved by
the National Socialist Movement (N.S.B.) which was liter-
ally hated by the Dutch as an alien body and besides, had
no able leaders who might have had a chance to win more
support.

For a long time, the attitude of the Union remained
wavering: one day it would come out with a firm adherence
to Dutch principles, next day it would pay lip service to
the German authorities. The break with the Germans finally
came with the German attack on Russia when the Netherlands Union refused to take sides in this conflict, stating:
"Although we and the people of the Netherlands recognize
in Communism one of our greatest enemies, it is at this
moment impossible for us to take sides in the Russo-German
conflict. Such a decision would only be made by our own
authorities, and in full liberty of action. . . . It is our deep-
est desire to grant to others what we consider our greatest
treasure: freedom of conscience."

Shortly after that, the Germans, realizing that they could
not get any real support from the Union, disbanded the
organization. It meant the end of a movement which had
served the purpose of creating greater unity among the
Dutch in a period of great discouragement, but which lacked

firm principles and had tried too much to compromise with national socialism. As the remaining political parties were disbanded shortly afterwards, Dutch political life had to go underground.

Immediately after the end of the war, another effort was made to break the Dutch party system and to create an all-embracing movement which, in its beginnings, did not intend to become a party. It has been said that there are certain trends in the People's Movement centering around the former underground newspaper, *Je Maintiendrai,* which originated in the Netherlands Union. There is a certain similarity between both movements in the socialistic ideas and in the stress upon the community spirit.

The newspaper, *Je Maintiendrai,* which had a considerable following among former Netherlands Union members, became the official organ of the People's Movement. In the leading group of the latter movement, we find again Dr. G. E. de Quay, one of the originators of the Netherlands Union. The criticism has been made that many leaders of the People's Movement refute remarks directed against the Union as if they were defending the same movement.

On the other hand, there are many groups in the People's Movement which were always hostile to the Union, and who would deny that there is any connection apart from the fact that a number of former Union members now belong to the People's Movement. It would, at least, be very difficult to see that anybody would at present back all the statements of the Union with its somewhat collaborationist flavor.

The People's Movement originated at a meeting held on September 13, 1945. Its roots reached far back, and can be traced to a meeting of six hostages in 1942 in the concentration camp at St. Michielsgestel. This small group had "found one another in a strong inner unrest about the impotence of political life in their native country, but above all about the lack of common spiritual foundation. They were convinced that a basis for collaboration had to be found which would give norms to direct concrete and radical changes of our society."*

When some members of this group were discharged in 1943, a concept of a program had already been prepared. They found contacts among the underground organizations, and then the group gradually grew.

Shortly after the liberation, the Movement decided to come out into the open as an organization founded by hostages and underground workers. It carries, in virtue of its origin, the sign of patriotic love of liberty as well as of resistance against Nazidom, and strengthened by suffering and struggle, is inspired by the will to lead our nation toward a strong and equitable social life based upon the responsibility of all its members. Further it is said that it is not only necessary to overcome the aftermath of war and occupation but to bring about a transition to a new solution for the inheritance of more than a century of industrial capitalism and the loss of spiritual authority and Christian morals.

"Our generation seems to have lost all real humanity and also regard for our fellow beings, mercy and justice. They have all become unholy phrases which do not buy you anything, either in the hard reality of the class struggle, or in our mechanized economic life."**

The N.V.B. (Nederlandsche Volksbeweging) has been created in the first place by the spiritual need of the Dutch people in all classes, a need caused by a deep seated demoralization which sees reconstruction as a individual, haphazard matter, not as an activity tested by definite and generally acknowledged norms. The innovation has to penetrate all realms of life: family and labor, national as well as international relations, politics and government. The development

---

* Ibid. p. 21.
** Cf. p. 20. "Voor het voetlicht. Schermerhorn en Banning over de N.V.B." Nederlandsche Volksbeweging, Amsterdam Centrum. No date.

of the personality can take place only under sound social conditions, and that entails the necessity of economic leadership of the community. Unfettered capitalism which created a hard, merciless spirit of individualism, materialism and hedonism has caused a decay of deeper spiritual values.

The N.V.B. believed that the political parties of the past had proved themselves incapable of overcoming the antithesis of social life, of finding a positive solution for the division of the nation. When the old political parties returned after the war, there was a danger that reconstruction would be considered mostly in terms of the past. The spokesmen of the N.V.B. saw the need for broader principles than the pre-war period had known. Although others considered the N.V.B. for the most part a political movement, the first and primary goal of the movement was beyond the political realm. It meant to be the crystallization point of the struggle for the renewal of authority, for inner obedience and moral discipline, elements which were essential for recovery according to the principles of all parties and all creeds.

Yet it was undeniable that the idea of one broad party, based upon the foundation of "personalistic socialism" would gradually lead to a political party, as happened in reality though in a slightly different way than the original N.V.B. leaders imagined.

The section of the original program of the N.V.B. which deals with the political renovation is not excessively clear. It is entitled (Section E of the program); *Renovation of the etatistic idea and reform of the democratic system in a personalistic spirit. Authority of the people in the organizations of economic and cultural life.*

Under the heading, "Necessity of a strong and efficient government," it reads:

"a) Recognition that a strong government truly develops through the collaboration between the executive organs of the government which express the factor of unity, and Parliament, which expresses the element of diversity.

"b) Reform of the government machine in such a way that differences between the cabinet members can be decided on short notice, for instance, by appeal to a small cabinet or a special cabinet group, with an increase in influence of the Prime Minister.

"c) Reform of the electoral and party system so that a limited number of parties would express the essential political trends."

Furthermore the program presses increased autonomy of the municipalities, obligatory publicity about the activities of political parties and their budgets, a more direct tie between the elector and the electee and a change in the system of proportional representation.

The practical reforms suggested by this program remain rather limited, and we must regard the N.V.B. as a philosophical movement which, in vain, attempted to create a number of principles upon which all parties could agree. It was obvious from the beginning that its socialist principles would attract a considerable following from the leftist parties and find some support among the left wings of the religious groups, but there was too much vagueness in its ethical principles to win adherence from the dogmatic groups of the right.

After the war, efforts were also made to create more unity among the Protestant parties and, for a brief period, a fusion of the Anti-Revolutionary and the Christian Historical parties was under consideration. It was visualized that there would be a large Catholic party, a great Democratic Socialist party, and a large Christian National party. For a short time a sort of federative collaboration between the two parties was reached but it was not possible to reach a fusion. The groups in the Christian Historical Union which were in favor of the People's Movement remained hostile to any collaboration with the Anti-Revolutionary group.

The Anti-Revolutionary Party, on the other hand, saw no possibility of cooperation with the N.V.B. The statement of the N.V.B., that the Christian antithesis was no longer of importance for the solution of our social problems was a horror to the Anti-Revolutionaries.

In a pamphlet by J. Schouten, *Party Formatie en Party Groepeering,* we read: "The Christian antithesis does not exist. This antithesis is the very fruit of disobedience to God. It is in its origin and application un-Christian.

"The antithesis is not acceptable to the Christians as a principle but they view it as a horrible reality, the result of the rejection of God's command. They have the calling to insist on a life in obedience to God's commands and to strive for a philosophy in keeping with the living ordinances. . . . There are Christians who limit Christianity to inner personal life and the life of the family and of the church in its institutional form. They see no relation between Christianity and politics, nor between Christianity and social life. Those Christians are wrong, in the opinion of the advocates of Christian political parties, according to the essence and nature of Christianity about the value and meaning of the Holy Scriptures and of God's commands."

On the basis of these reflections, the author rejects the philosophy of the N.V.B. and comes to the conclusion that there is no possibility of any collaboration.

In Catholic circles the situation was somewhat different. In the *Christofoor* group, known by the name of a newspaper it published, there was considerable sympathy for the aims of the N.V.B. It was inspired by neo-Thomistic philosophy and the system of Salazar.

According to this system, the Prime Minister alone is responsible to Parliament while the directives for his actions are contained in the principles of a large majority party. In the underground press during the occupation, there was already considerable dissatisfaction with the party system as it existed before the war. The reasoning was generally somewhat along the following lines: "The large pre-war parties have all developed in order to reach certain equality for different groups of the population. They served the purpose of political emancipation. Now that this process has been completed and that general suffrage and equal rights for the religious schools have been obtained, now that labor is certain of its place in political life and the Roman Catholics have equal rights with all other Dutch citizens, the old parties can result only in a hindrance for fuller development. A new basis has to be found that is adjusted to the demands which the coming period will make upon the parties. The old party system was petrified, it has become a purpose in itself. Instead of a purpose, it should again become a means."*

Also in other Catholic groups there was sympathy in the beginning for the N.V.B. "There is no doubt that most [Catholics] will subscribe wholeheartedly to the program [of the N.V.B.] as it has been announced. Many, however, for historical reasons and out of prudence will want the continuation of their own political group. They will propagate in the N.V.B. the special opinions of their party and in their party the program of the People's Movement and its ideas of collaboration. I can visualize, however, that from the beginning, or when a definite choice of party becomes imperative, many younger (and older) Catholics will prefer the N.V.B. also as a political group."**

The forces within the Catholic population which were strong for new solutions, attempted in several other directions to break the principle of the necessity of one Catholic Party. It was felt that the formation of the Catholics as one

* Quoted from *Het Parool* p. 43, "De illegale pers over na oorlogsche problemen," Van Gorcum & Comp., N. V. Assen.

** P. 39, W. I. M. Van Gent, *De Nederlandsche Katholieken en het vraagstuk eener nieuwe party groepeering.*

political group was no longer a necessity and could not be derived from Catholic philosophy as a logical conclusion. The remark was also made that the creation of a political program by deduction from a few philosophical principles was no longer applicable in our modern times. The need was felt for empirical thinking which considers matters on an historical basis and takes natural growth into consideration. For practical politics, historical feeling and psychological insight are as necessary as philosophical depth to which must be added the political intuition which "distinguishes the impossible from the extraordinary."

The historical factors which united the Catholics into one party still have considerable strength as was proved sufficiently by the fact that ultimately the N.V.B. did not succeed in getting a larger Catholic group under its banner while the "Catholic State Party" continued to be the only Catholic political organization. It can now be analyzed whether or not this return to the former set-up is a result of the uncertainty of the war years; whether the reasons which caused the Catholic party to develop into such a formidable organization are still too strong or whether it is simply too deeply rooted to be displaced by other organizational structures. Perhaps, and this may have been the strongest factor, the emancipation of the Catholic part of the population has not progressed far enough to give the Catholics the inner security necessary to abandon their own organization. As a Roman Catholic priest said recently:

"Only when Nijmegen and Tilburg [the Catholic universities] have existed for fifty years, will there no longer be any need for the Catholic State Party."

There is considerable uncertainty, however, in Catholic circles how the Catholic members of a large majority party would conduct themselves in case subjects came up which would be at variance with Catholic principles as, for instance, eugenics or the problem of the natural increase of the family.

The lack of empirical thinking remains a great obstacle to practical political collaboration in the Netherlands. As long as the major parties continue to have a definite philosophy, they can arrive at a working agreement on concrete matters but not at any desirable arrangement which would require a common foundation. Only if these groups which no longer see any necessary connection between religion and politics gain a majority, could such an arrangement ultimately be feasible.

The current distinction between "democratic" and "non-democratic" groups has not penetrated the Netherlands very deeply as democracy in a political sense has been generally accepted while democracy as a philosophy is somewhat too vague to compete with earlier and deeper philosophical thinking.

At the moment, the majority of the desires for change have submerged again, but much of it may return at a later date when the more immediate problems of the post-war period have been solved.

Among the aims on which most post-war planners agreed, social security took a high place. Assurance of the permanence of the opportunity to work is a major concern which cannot be solved by public works or institutions like a labor service. It is felt that a minimum standard of living should be safeguarded for everybody, with the inclusion of a general pension plan. The ideas of Beveridge have not lacked a following in the Netherlands.

Big fortunes come in for considerable criticism and it has been suggested repeatedly that a high capital levy would be the best means to reduce the staggering public debt. It is assumed that capital formation will take place from the normal incomes via the insurance companies. The idea of a minimum income has been mentioned but present taxation measures are not too far removed from achieving that goal already.

Production according to needs is a theme which occurred frequently in the underground press. Yet, the desire for equalization and standardization which is dominant in so many utterances will be a difficult point for a nation whose commercial position in the world is of such great importance.

Among the numerous suggestions for economic reforms, there are hardly any which do not propagate a regulated economy. Corporative ideas of various types are met in Catholic as well as in labor publications. Socialization of the main means of production is a favorite subject in leftist circles.

It must be considered fortunate, however, that as soon as the war was ended, the inherent liberal trends of the Dutch came to the fore. Whether it is to be regretted or not that Dutch political life was reestablished very much according to the pattern of the past, is an open question. There is more political and economic skill in the old groups than there is in the new ones, and the stability shown so far, as well as the quick economic reconstruction, are on the positive side of the ledger. A reconstruction period needs concrete thinking, and is not the proper time for the introduction of far-reaching reforms.

In comparison with the pre-war period, the simplification of the structure of Dutch political life has proved to be of minor significance. Instead of the twenty parties which participated in the elections of 1937, the elections of April 9, 1946, showed that eleven parties were putting up candidates: The Anti-Revolutionary Party, the Labor Party, Protestant Union, The Catholic People's Party, Reformed State Party, the Christian Historical Union, the Communist Party of the Netherlands, the Freedom Party, the Netherlands Bellamy Party, Independent Party (group Lopez), and the Christian Democratic Party. The electoral age was lowered from 25 to 23, partly in view of the attitude of the younger generation under the occupation. The success of these parties at the polls was as follows:

Labor	28.31%	29 seats in the Lower House					
Catholics	30.81%	32	"	" "	"	"	
Anti-Revolutionary . .	12.90%	13	"	" "	"	"	
Christian Historical ..	7.84%	8	"	" "	"	"	
Communist	10.57%	10	"	" "	"	"	
Freedom	6.41%	6	"	" "	"	"	
Reformed State	2.14%	2	"	" "	"	"	
Protestant Union . . .	0.67%	0	"	" "	"	"	
Bellamy	0.23%	0	"	" "	"	"	
Independent	0.12%	0	"	" "	"	"	

Out of eleven parties which submitted lists, eight saw their candidates elected which means, at any rate, a sizeable decrease compared with the all-time high of 54 parties in the early thirties.

We will give a survey of the program of the leading parties in order to gain an exact picture of existing differences and possible greater unification in the future.

From the program of the Anti-Revolutionary Party we mention the following points:

1. Maintenance of authority. The government has to be constantly aware of being the servant of God to the benefit of the people.

2. Overseas territories. Reconstruction with force and wisdom of legal authority in the Indies. Reconstruction of government based on law and further development in that direction.

The policy is to be directed toward strong encouragement of the development of the community for the benefit of the population, and toward speedy attainment of complete autonomy, however with definite maintenance of the unity of the Kingdom.

From the economic program we mention the following points:

Subheading II—*Socialization, directed economy and government organization of economic life.*

We are AGAINST:

A) Socialization that means the gradual abolition of private property of the soil or means of production.

B) Directed economy, namely, the permanent direction of the economy by government . . .

Subheading III—*Economic cycles.*

Insofar as it is possible for the government to prevent or alleviate economic crises without taking over control of economic life, such a policy should be encouraged and supported.

The Christian Historical Union brings the following points of interest in its program:

A) The belief that God is sovereign over all creation, urges us to attempt to understand His will and to carry out His commands, also in the political and social realm.

B) The authority of the government has to be respected and maintained because it finds its origin in God.

The program also lists 18 "urgent points" of which we mention the following:

POINT 6:—The government should recognize an interchurch institute which can deal officially with the government and to which the government can address itself in regard to problems which touch the spiritual and moral well-being of the nation.

POINT 11:—The internal matters of the Overseas Territories should be delegated as much as possible to competent organs in these territories. Native talent should be given ample opportunity in official position.

Missionary activities and religious education should receive complete freedom of development . . .

It is remarkable that the Christian Historical Union takes a much more conservative stand in regard to the Indies than the Anti-Revolutionary Party which, in spite of its strict principles, breathes a spirit of considerable depth.

The Communist Party of the Netherlands has a less start-ling program than one might expect. Under the headline *Reconstruction, Organization, Production,* it states:

1) Increase of production, work for everybody. The econ-omy should be directed mainly to the production of food, clothing and mass consumption goods.

2) Retraining of workers by the government on a vast scale with adequate compensation.

3) Energetic and efficient direction of the economy by the government.

> a. Nationalization of the banks, the mines, the large port installations, the shipping companies and airlines, the metal and shipbuilding industries, and Philips concern [*sic!*], the textile industry, the Unilever and other monopolistic enterprises, as well as insurance companies, savings and loan banks."

In the section *For the Unity of a Free Holland and a Free Indonesia* the following points deserve attention:

1. Complete abolition in form and spirit of the colonial regime in Indonesia, Surinam and Curacao. Withdrawal of British and Dutch armed forces from Indonesia.

2. No transfer of Dutch draftees or volunteers without their permission to Indonesia in accordance with the funda-mental law. Cancellation of the Royal Decree regarding this matter . . .

3. The goal should be to reach voluntary collaboration in every respect between Indonesia and the Netherlands in a commonwealth with equal civic rights for Indonesians and Netherlanders in both countries. . . .

In the program of the Catholic People's Party* we find the following salient points:

Emergency Program

I Strengthening of the spiritual and moral foundations of national life.

> 1. To rebuild the deeply shattered public morale, it is necessary in the first place, that the government with-

---

* The name for the former Catholic State Party

in the confines of its task increase the respect for God and religion, and defend and protect the value of the human personality, family, authority and the nation.

5. In regard to marriage, it is recognized that divorce is a disaster for the community. In consequence of this, it should be considered to demand a waiting period in the case of a request for divorce and to grant the divorce only if the reasons stated have been proved.

7. Strong measures should be taken to secure the recognition and application of moral principles as they are indispensable for a well regulated community life. Especially measures should be taken against corruption in all forms, usury, the public advocation of neo-Malthusianism and excesses in the field of amusements.

Reconstruction and expansion of the constitutional structure of the Kingdom

The Catholic People's Party advocates the liquidation of colonial relationships, the speedy attainment of a constitutional reform whereby, on the basis of equality, the various parts of the Kingdom collaborate as foreseen in Queen Wilhelmina's statement of December 6th, 1942.

The ideas of the People's Movement which originated the Labor Party have been dealt with at some length so that it suffices to enumerate some of their tenets in regard to matters which were listed under the programs of some of the other parties.

In regard to the Overseas Territories, the Labor Party's program states:

Recognition of the right of self-determination of the population of the Overseas Territories.

In the near future colonial relations should be liquidated, and, on the basis of voluntary collaboration, a constitutional reform should be caused but in order to attain a coordinated structure of the Kingdom, on the foundation of full equality of all parts of the realm.

The economic principles of the Labor Party are definitely on the progressive side and include:

A plan for national prosperity in order to achieve security for all on the basis of a decent standard of living for all.

Socialization of mines, of the bank issues, of public utilities as well as of certain monopolistic enterprises.

a) Government control on the credit system.

b) Democratization of economic enterprises.

c) Protection of the interests of the consumer.

Special care for the protection and fostering of sound smaller enterprises within the framework of a general social policy aimed at the commonweal.

The Freedom Party, the offspring of the former Liberals, presents a fairly conservative program. It advocates:

Unity of the Kingdom and within the Kingdom autonomy of the parts. Continuation of the constitutional parliamentary monarchy under the House of Orange. Maintenance of the rights of Parliament and improvement of its procedure in the preparation and execution of laws; institutions which have developed through the free interplay of social forces should be given a role.

In the economic sphere, collaboration between free organizations of employers and workers is seen as the best solution while socialization is regarded as detrimental because it gives too much power to the government. Monopolies are condemned and free enterprise is interpreted as protection of the rights of the small entrepeneur.

This kaleidoscopic survey cannot give a complete picture of the aims of the various parties, but it may help to show the fundamental trends of Dutch politics. It makes clear, perhaps, that apart from the communist parties, the differences in policy are more in degree than in principle although the philosophic foundations of the various parties still seem relatively far apart. They all acclaim Christian ethics, but, while Christianity has a rather concrete meaning for the Protestant and Catholic parties, it remains a somewhat vague code of behavior for the others. Although the Liberal party itself has lost considerably in influence in the Netherlands, there are many elements in the different programs which definitely betray the spirit of nineteenth century Dutch liberalism.

On the whole, Dutch political life breathes a spirit of moderation and progressiveness although the variety of principles and programs may make it somewhat slow and cumbersome. It is a firm foothold of democracy in Western Europe, steeped in a tradition of self-reliance and independence which should make it a valuable element of stability in a potentially still explosive Europe. Whether a further simplification of its political life is possible, and whether there might be a possibility of breaking through the religious divisions in its political life, remains to be seen. Modern political thinking may prove to lack sufficient philosophical roots. Perhaps it is preferable to have principles based upon deeper convictions although one cannot help but wish that these deeper convictions could be brought to one common denominator. The benefit of mankind as a whole might be the modern principle on which all creeds and systems could agree. Even absolute principles, however, applied with moderation and fairness, would be capable of achieving the same result of a harmonious civilization. The smaller countries can make a great contribution to the future of the world by showing that the art of living together has, to them, become a living concept.

CHAPTER V*

Economic Conditions

WHEN HOLLAND WAS liberated by the Allied Armies in May 1945, its joy in freedom regained was somewhat tempered by a realization of the vast losses that the country had suffered. Especially in the eight months which elapsed between the liberation of Maastricht in September, 1944, and the final surrender of the Germans in the West on May 5, 1945, the enemy engaged in an orgy of destruction.

The chaos which the government found in May was not comparable to the conditions of September, 1944. It had been possible, however, to prepare in the southern Netherlands for the liberation of the West. The work that was achieved in the first six months can truly be called amazing, in view of the incredible difficulties resulting from disorganization, flooding, an almost complete lack of communications, and the like. There were neither raw materials nor coal, nor any ships to transport the most essential goods.

After the liberation, the first problem was the importation of foodstuffs. Up to May 31, 1945, 8,000 tons were imported; a month later this amount had risen to more than 260,000 tons. In the months of July and August this figure increased to well over 1,049,000 tons. Through October 20 the figure stands at 1,809,000 tons.

This may sound simple, but, to realize the enormous problem, one has only to consider that a freight car takes ten tons and a truck three. In addition to this, internal production was stepped up immediately, and after May 5, 1945,

---

* Reprinted with kind permission of the editor from the "Foreign Commerce Weekly," May 15, 1946.

millions of pounds of potatoes came from the eastern provinces. If we look at it in terms of calories per inhabitant, we get a better picture: from 450 calories a day in May, 1945, the rations rose in less than 6 months to 2,200 calories, much beyond the average of Europe then. (Before the war the average consumption in the Netherlands stood at 2,800-3,000 calories daily.) And this happened while there was actual starvation in the cities of the Western Netherlands before the liberation, with the death rate well over 250 per cent of that in 1944, when food conditions had been far from inspiring. The relatively favorable situation was due to the fact that the Netherlands Government in London started purchasing food as early as 1941.

In less vital matters, the improvement was slower—but it was, nevertheless, substantial. Apart from food, clothing and shoes constituted the No. 2 problem of the Dutch people. To start the Dutch textile industry, two things were needed —coal and raw materials.

Yet, by September it was possible to begin the distribution of textile goods on a very limited scale to the people of the so-called "emergency regions." In order to achieve this, everything was bought which the world market offered: Finished products, semi-finished products, and raw materials. The figures indicate the textile imports following the general liberation.

May 1945	367	Tons
June	3,922	"
July	10,584	"
August	9,258	"
September	5,416	"

Even more difficult than the matter of textiles was the problem of shoes. At the end of the war the Dutch were walking on torn and dilapidated shoes. The Allied Armies gave aid to many people in the South, but in the North the Dutch themselves stepped in as soon as possible. By July,

1945, 592 tons of leather and shoes were imported, by October about 9,915 tons. Shoe rationing was organized on a regional basis which made it possible to supply 340,000 pairs of shoes in the first four months to districts comprising about 1,400,000 people. As soon as the districts have all been supplied, national rationing will take place on the basis of 600,000 pairs of shoes a month. This production is expected in the very near future.**

The next priority had to be given to housing. After the liberation, investigation showed that 80,000 houses in the Netherlands had been destroyed, 35,000 heavily damaged, and 270,000 lightly damaged. It took only three months to restore 280,000 houses in the two categories last named. Emergency houses were set up in a relatively short time, reaching a figure of about 5,000 at the end of 1945, but there proved to be very bad bottlenecks in building—lumber (it sounds familiar) being the worst one. Of 375,000 cubic meters of lumber ordered abroad, only a small percentage arrived. Glass? There was not even enough to repair the damaged houses in the city of The Hague alone. The end of 1945 saw the arrival of 60,000 square meters of glass from Belgium, and more is expected monthly as an exchange for the products which Holland exports to its neighbor countries.

There is no window-glass production in Holland, although some factories make special emergency glass and more can be made when the used X-ray plates from the hospitals are utilized. Building will take time, but 1946 had on its program 10,000 new houses and the repair of thousands of others.***

In 1945, before the liberation, there was no light in the Netherlands. A tiny oil lamp was all any person had. There was no electricity—which meant that there were no lights, no streetcars, no doorbells, no irons, no vacuum cleaners. Now,

---

** Now every person is entitled to at least one pair a year.
*** The program for 1947 foresees 28,00 new houses.

everywhere in the Netherlands, there is electricity again. there is light in the homes—the streetcars run (though on a limited scale)—there are electric trains—theatres and movies play to capacity audiences. As an example of the work involved, it may be pointed out that electric power lines connecting cities roughly 60 miles apart had been damaged in 1,500 places.

During the war, the Germans took electricity from Holland. Lately the roles have been reversed, and Holland gets about 40,000 kilowatts from the Ruhr region. Cooking again takes place on gas—as was the custom in pre-war Holland—as a result of substantial imports of gas cokes from the United States.

Better than anticipated was the availability of motorcars. Before the war, Holland had 3,500,000 bicycles and 300,000 cars—one bicycle to every 2.6 inhabitants. When the Germans departed, only 7,000 trucks were left out of 48,000. Repairs and imports boosted this number to 30,000 while 29,000 passenger cars reappeared on the road. Oil products were imported between May and October to a total of 1,163,-000 tons, and just recently the price of gasoline was reduced to almost the pre-war level. While the import of gasoline in February, 1945, stood at 610 tons, it had risen to 431,000 tons in August. Twelve thousand tires came in during the first few months, and, by the end of 1945, Holland's traffic amounted to two-thirds of the pre-war figures.

A sad, but very impressive, story is provided by the railroads. The Germans left utter desolation behind: ninety per cent of the electric wiring was gone; 181 railroad bridges had been destroyed; 20 per cent of the stations were damaged; 40 per cent of the signal installations; 350 locomotives gone (out of 866); 1,879 passenger cars stolen, out of a total of 2,804. The story of the freight cars repeats the same dismal tale even more convincingly: 25,117 cars gone, out of 29,619.

The railroaders lost no time in getting back to work. In

October, 1945, 2,000 miles of tracks were in use again, and once more one could travel everywhere in Holland, although often by devious routes and in unheated cars. In the West, between Rotterdam, The Hague, and Amsterdam, rail traffic was almost back to normal when 1946 made its bow. Cars and locomotives came back from Germany in small numbers, but they came. Today a timetable of the Dutch railroads has almost the qualities of an absorbing serial, because every issue tells the prospective traveler of more trains.

Holland's canals were also in sad shape when the war ended. Many locks had been blown up, and numerous boats had been sunk by the enemy to impede the recovery. The Twente Canal, in the textile district, alone had 23 destroyed bridges, and only the help of the Canadian Army made it possible to clear a number of the obstacles. The big rivers had all been cleared by the end of 1945, and there are no more hindrances to normal traffic on the Rhine.

Although the story may become monotonous, we will repeat a few more instances of the rapid economic recovery of Holland. Of about 30 airfields, only a few were still usable when the usurper left. But work on the airfields was started immediately, and before the end of the war, airfields in the southern Netherlands served for attacks on the enemy in the North.

The repair of Schiphol Airport at Amsterdam was undertaken with great energy. All runways, including the fog runway, have been repaired, and planes arrive daily from all corners of the globe, including New York and the Netherlands Indies. New airfields have been projected, and the one in Zeeland is nearing completion.

Postal, telegraph, and telephone services, from a condition of almost non-existence in May, 1945, have reached a practically normal situation by this time, although it will take time before the level has been reached which recent plans foresee.

Similar stories of reconstruction could be told about the bridges, harbors, flooded areas—which all were dry by the end of 1945—agriculture, industry and trade. It may suffice to record that, on the average, the Netherlands industries have regained between 60 and 70 per cent of their pre-war capacity and are engaged in exports so far as internal conditions permit, in order to build up foreign exchange.

Before the war, Holland's balance of trade was typical for a creditor nation, always showing a large surplus of imports over exports, the difference being made up by such items as investments abroad, income from shipping, and income from harbor facilities.

In the period of reconstruction, Holland's balance of payments will necessarily continue to show a deficit. Necessary imports for 1946 are estimated at 3,000,000,000 guilders. This huge amount is caused by the need of importing machinery, raw materials, and equipment, though it must be taken into account that prices are higher than in 1940. Exports for 1946 are estimated at about 1,000,000,000 guilders* which would leave a deficit of 2,000,000,000 guilders. Among the main export articles at present (listed according to value) are: Seeds, radio articles and electric light bulbs, wool, seed potatoes, iron, flower bulbs and flowers, fish, edible oils, pulse, groundnut cakes, triple, vacuum cleaners. The main countries of destination in February, 1946, were Belgium, France, Switzerland, the United Kingdom, Sweden and Spain, whereas in December exports went to Belgium, the United Kingdom, France, Sweden, and the United States.

The satisfactory rate of recovery was stimulated to a considerable extent by the "financial purge" which gave Holland's economy a relatively great element of stability.

In September, 1945, all currency (bank notes as well as treasury notes) were withdrawn, while all bank balances

---

* This goal was almost reached. Import figures for December stood at 127,000,000 guilders.

were frozen. Each individual received no more than 10 guilders in new notes in the first week. From that crucial period on, a gradual "de-freezing" process set in which is still continuing, although the ratio between "free" and "blocked" money has changed continuously in favor of the former. By these measures Finance Minister Pieter Lieftinck has succeeded in reducing note circulation from well over 5,000,-000,000 guilders to between 1,000,000,000 and 2,000,000,000. Although the ratio between money-in-circulation and available goods is considerably higher than before the war, it compares favorably with other countries and has tended to re-establish Holland's reputation for financial stability.

Nevertheless, there is some concern about the increase in wholesale prices, as reflected in the following table.

ITEM	Wholesale 1940	Wholesale JANUARY 1946
General index	130.6	236.1
Foodstuffs	121.4	192.7
Raw materials	263.2	258.9
Finished articles	126.4	245.7

The fact, however, that price fluctuations in the Netherlands have remained within reasonable limits gives a sound foundation for its import and export program. It is evident that imports will continue for some time to consist of basic materials, as is evident from the following statistics.

IMPORTS (BY PRINCIPAL COMMODITIES)

COMMODITY	JANUARY 1946 (long tons)	FEBRUARY 1946 (long tons)
Wheat	107,044	54,021
Coal	218,360	217,744
Artificial fertilizers	43,918	35,947
Petroleum	23,939	23,032
Oil	26,794	16,747
Gasoline	17,152	31,508
Wood	58,786	37,061

The most important countries of origin are given in the following table, showing in long tons the amount of goods each supplied to the Netherlands during January and February:

COUNTRY OF ORIGIN	JANUARY 1946	FEBRUARY 1946
United States	228,623	284,423
Germany	138,907	129,607
Belgium and Luxemburg	102,772	115,694
Curacao	53,272	58,282
Great Britain	62,057	40,944
Sweden	75,013	29,838

Netherlands exports in February were valued at 24,000,000 guilders, as compared with 18,400,000 guilders in January. The comparative values of the most important exports, all of which showed a rise from January to February are given below.

COMMODITY	JANUARY 1946 Guilders	FEBRUARY 1946 Guilders
Seeds	1,100,000	4,200,000
Seed potatoes	700,000	1,300,000
Bulbs, Plants, etc.......	500,000	1,200,000
Radio parts	160,000	2,100,000

Exports were distributed mainly in the manner shown below:

COUNTRY OF DESTINATION	JANUARY 1946 Guilders	FEBRUARY 1946 Guilders
France	1,100,000	2,800,000
Switzerland	2,500,000	2,600,000
Great Britain	2,400,000	2,100,000
Sweden	2,300,000	1,700,000
Spain	......	1,000,000

So far as exports are concerned, Holland hopes to regain

partly its former exports and to develop a number of new products, mostly of an industrial nature. A publication of the Economic Information Service in The Hague gives the following products as expectedly available for exportation in the course of 1946: Cattle, fish, cheese, dairy produce, horticulture seeds, agricultural seeds, fresh fruits, fruit pulp, preserved fruit, fresh vegetables, preserved vegetables, seed potatoes, cut flowers, flower bulbs, nursery products, cocoa butter, powder and chocolate products, gin, farina products, straw, willow-hoops, cigars, metalware, chemical products, paints, lacquers and varnishes, artificial horn products, linoleum, medicines, coal-tar products, printed matter, wooden ware, precious stones, objects of applied art, earthenware, bricks and tiles, crystal, musical instruments, toys, paintings and antiques, carpets, textiles, pig iron, gold and silverware, tungsten and molybdenum, wire, ships and boats, electrical products, and household articles.

In pre-war days the Netherlands and the Kingdom's Overseas Territories contributed to the following imports of the United States, in some cases to a substantial degree: crude rubber, coffee, cane sugar, tin, furs, distilled liquors, raw hides and skins, diamonds, copper, unmanufactured tobacco, fertilizer materials, fish, burlap, cocoa beans, tea, coal-tar products, fuel oils and unfinished distillates, industrial chemicals, art works, spices, cheese, drugs, herbs, leaves and roots, rayon, leather, books, woven wool fabrics, cotton cloth, sisal and henequen fiber, unmanufactured cotton, bristles, sausage casings, pottery, copra, essential oils, palen oil, farina products, platinum ores, shellac and other resins, medicinal preparations, logs, wool carpets, wool wearing apparel, manila, hats of straw, bauxite, jute and jute butts, aluminum, agricultural machinery and implements, rags and other paper stock, jelutong and guttas, oats, paraffin and paraffin wax.

Up to the present, foreign exchange shortages and the problems of the internal economy have made it necessary to maintain a strict system of import and export licenses. How-ever, it is the principle of the Dutch Government to return to unfettered private trade as soon as conditions permit. It could not be said that there exists an over-all plan to develop the trade relations of the Netherlands. The idea is more to stimulate trade through a number of treaties, many of which have been concluded. An agreement with Great Britain is under negotiation, while trade with Canada and Belgium has developed very satisfactorily. The Netherlands is pre-pared to give Belgium a monopoly on glass production, while Holland would export a variety of products among which dairy products would be the most important. A trade agree-ment with Czechoslovakia was signed on December 20th; it provides for Dutch exports of seed potatoes, vegetables, flower seeds, flax products, iron and steel products and radio prod-ucts, while imports will consist of iron and steel products, machine tools and other machinery, automobiles, bicycles, textiles, porcelain floor tiles, glass, heat resistant stonework, chemical products, malt, hops, and clover seed.

Trade agreements were also concluded with Italy and Switzerland, while negotiations are under way with Norway and Portugal. The commercial fair which was recently held at Utrecht was a great success from the point of view of at-tendance and exhibitors. The actual volume of trade was still small, but great hopes were held out for the autumn fair. The Dutch hope that the Utrecht fair may gain the signifi-cance which Leipzig held prior to the war.

The great activity in Holland shows that the Dutch realize how important *foreign trade* is in their economic structure. Their purpose to develop as many contacts as possible shows considerable foresight, it is felt, and the famous "stubborn-ness" of the nation, as well as the Netherlanders' innate abil-ity to trade, augurs well for the future of a people who know that, from now on, the prosperity of one country depends more than ever on that of others.

CHAPTER VI

Long Range Economic Problems

A PERIOD OF DURESS and privations leaves the mind with a wider range—although one too immediately based upon emotions—than normal times. Thus, it is not a surprise that in the liberated countries, there is a lot of thinking of an emotional nature which changes rapidly from extreme optimism to deep pessimism and has a predilection for far-reaching schemes without too much attention to details or possible realization.

In dealing with the programs of the political parties, we had opportunity to observe that there is frequently a certain vagueness and a trend toward general philosophical statements which betray the influence of five years of German thinking.

Especially in regard to economic problems, there is a departure from traditional Dutch thinking which may mean a desirable innovation or which may imply the working with new phrases whose applicability to Dutch conditions have not been sufficiently considered.

There is good reason for the Dutch to reconsider their economic position as several of its former mainstays are of doubtable strength, but whether a change in orientation should lead to a change in principles is a matter which belongs to an entirely different level. Too often the human mind has shown an inclination to react to a change of circumstances with a change in philosophy, and these philosophies are often dragged along when the conditions that caused them long cease to exist. It could be argued that any systematic philosophy carries in it the reflection of certain conditions and that its claim to generaly validity is an expression of ignorance in regard to its own motivation. It would be interesting to investigate what a sociological analysis of philosophical thinking would reveal, but it is hardly the place to go into this matter in this book.

It is tempting, however, to reflect that many of the world's ponderous thinkers did not do more than defend the interest of a given social group although one cannot but bow to the width and depth of their arguments and the thoroughness of their thoughts. Today, however, one would be inclined to doubt the value of a work which claimed to present a philosophic system.

It is not easy to explain why this attitude should exist in most of us. Is it because the modern world has become so complex that any attempt to interpret it in its entirety would necessarily carry an undertone of insincerity? Or is it because we have become mentally tired and skeptical and would not be able to bring ourselves to an intelligent discussion of the underlying forces of our present form of civilization?

A third possibility would be that we are facing the most difficult of all problems, namely, to stabilize the human mind for a long period and, therefore, we have a strong aversion to uprooting it while at the same time we are trying to smooth it out. Once the machine has been put in working order, however, someone will have to furnish a written explanation of it which should have a sufficient amount of correctness to ring true to the public.

In Europe we can observe that people struggle with general philosophical notions without being able to transfer them to a practical level while in the United States the reverse seems to be true. There, practical problems are solved magnificently, but one is forever waiting for an acceptable ideological superstructure which remains conspicuously absent. Philosophy, literature, art, in their great periods, have grown out of the problems of the people but have not been grafted on from other civilizations, or at least they were ultimately completely assimilated.

The great and simple lines of modern thinking have within them the possibility of amazing variety, depth and richness. We have had both the variety and the simple lines but the combination of the two has come to naught. What we are striving for is the renewal of a classical civilization which, within a simple and clear framework, could show the same astounding love for reality in all its colors. We modern people are hesitating on the brink of two worlds unable to reconcile the wealth of material creation with our atrophied minds, unable to understand that culture is but a way of giving permanence and color to the underlying pattern of life which remains fundamentally the same although the accentuation and relative importance of contributing factors change.

Our thinking and our art belong to a different period than our present world. Instead of leading the world or attempting to do so, they lag behind and are far from giving the inner liberation which the function of philosophy or art should be. To wonder about things is the beginning of philosophy as well as art, but one could hardly say that picking up a periodical or a book nowadays opens up any interesting horizons." The reporting of everyday life can have significance if it brings out any fundamental disturbing quality about this life, but not if it amounts to a phonographic reproduction of nauseating sameness.

Whether the taste of the masses requires vulgarization is entirely a moot question. It has been proved that good music draws, in the long run, more audiences than entertainment music, and the same holds true in other fields of endeavor.

Let us try to apply the patterns of a few simple principles projected against reality to the economic problems of the Netherlands.

There are still two schools of thought. The trained ones

who, from their hiding places, still cry occasionally that wealth is the aim of our economic system and sigh for the days of Adam Smith when more workers continually produced more needles until the world became a nightmare of needles with the capitalist who got 100 per cent of one cent out of each needle sitting on top. Capitalism and the capitalist did their duty in a world which was changing from a lower to a higher standard of living. Now that we are trying to stabilize the world, no more of him.

That is approximately the way the masses of the people feel about things. But, as we are in a period of reconstruction, the capitalist pushed out of the front door sneaks back through the kitchen entrance. The picture in Holland is even more complicated.

The distinction in Holland between "nice people" and "not-so-nice people" is still tremendously strong. Very consistently, a distinction has been made between nice capitalists and not-so-nice capitalists. This is a great departure from the old times when they were all above suspicion. At present, those who had money before the war are all right, while those who made it during the war are not.

Ethical distinctions made this way can always be easily attacked theoretically, but there is no doubt that this decision reflects the way a lot of people feel about this matter. But these restrictive measures, which are never entirely successful, also created a distinction between "white" and "black" capital.

This leads us back to our starting point, namely that a period of reconstruction requires considerable capital, even if all concerned agree that the ultimate goal is the satisfaction of reasonable needs and not production for profit. In order to prevent private enterprise from making undue profits in times of emergency, the government has to step in and exercise extensive control over the reconstruction program.

This, in turn, slows the recovery process and causes the continuation of a black market, not only a market where consumer goods are offered for sale, but which offers capital and services. Thus, the process of reconstruction is made more nearly even but, also, slower. We have this same phenomenon in every field of modern civilization. Our civilization, for a number of reasons, creates numerous controls while these controls have the effect of stabilizing matters and of levelling them off at the same time.

As this trend is general in the world, there need be no fear in making the exchange of speed for stability, and the levelling off process can only be regretted by those who were educated for a world of greater mental differentiation.

Thus, we fear that those who grumble in the Netherlands about government interference will continue to grumble for a few more years as they would hestitate themselves to accept the responsibility for the return to a free economy. It remains a major problem, however, to decrease control measures gradually, and this, again, is a problem which is common to most countries, but is more intense in the liberated ones.

Again we must make it clear to ourselves what we are trying to control or why. Do we want a return to a profit economy? Many would undoubtedly answer, "Yes," with a poor reply to a poorly worded question. There has never been a really free economy, and the question which we have been debating for half a century is how extensive government control should be. The question put this way becomes a great deal simpler.

Hardly anybody wants a return to a pure "police state" which only safeguards the life and property of its citizens and provides them with an absolute minimum of education. Governments nowadays are supposed to provide stability and security to their citizens, which means that a normal citizen has the right to a job and to adequate social legislation to protect him in periods of sickness, disability, old age or unemployment.

The system of individual responsibility which may have led to high achievement in a period of expansion is of such manifest unfairness under stabilized conditions that it does not even deserve discussion. Extensive social measures mean a more even distribution of income and, thereby, a more even demand.

A stabilized demand would do a great deal toward absorbing economic booms and depressions while taxation is another powerful tool in the hands of the government to prevent economic upheavals. Psychologically, we can only explain booms and depressions in a period of expansion when a hitch in the development occurs which leads to temporary stagnation. There is no reason to believe that there is any necessity for permanent economic disturbances although a normal economic growth may cause minor frictions at times.

The greatest danger at present is that excessive and unnecessary restrictions and controls will be maintained. Control of prices can only be a temporary measure as it immediately creates a black market, and is a palliative measure which can be justified only in times of emergency.

A fair wage and salary policy will automatically exercise sufficient control over our economic system, and beyond that a return to the hallowed principles of liberty is the only acceptable solution. The more people are directly concerned with the production and distribution of goods, the more there will be of them, and unnecessary controls mean not only a detour in production but also the creation of a class which has no real productive function. Controls should be abandoned as soon as production has become sufficient to meet a normal demand. From then on the ancient laws of supply and demand are certain to keep matters balanced as long as the demand is kept on a fairly even keel.

Attempts to extend government control by increased nationalization seems to offer no solution. Services for the public good like the post and telegraph have been operated by governments in most countries for a long time, as were railroads and public utilities. Theoretically speaking, the public good is concerned in every economic activity and would by such a claim open the gate to complete socialization. With a restricted profit motive, it becomes hard to see what the advantages of nationalization are, especially since it paralyzes international trade.

It should never be forgotten that government, meaning a group of people, can never make the population, meaning another group of people, do certain things. They can only threaten them with certain unpleasant consequences in case they do not conform to a pattern, and even this is theoretical. Let us assume that the government has assigned a strictly defined task to each individual. Could it expect the individuals to observe these regulations, even if a whole class of government officials were active in checking the observation of the rules? It should be kept in mind that the people, themselves, elect the governments and will hardly be in favor of excessive controls. Too much government defeats itself at the price of tremendous misery as the Nazis have demonstrated so clearly.

Why were certain industries nationalized? Purely because in times of a free economy they would have yielded excessive profits to unscrupulous capitalists. As this argument is no longer valid, extension of nationalization has become a hobbyhorse of overzealous theoretical socialists. It lacks a real purpose, and is merely another effort of political parties to create a state within the state.

If the world has to choose between regimentation and liberty, let it choose liberty because regimentation is a dead end street. Extensive controls breed extensive abuses, and they again require new controls on an unending road which leads nowhere.

The world is populated with two billion people who all want to find their own way to happiness. They will accept a system which provides the greatest happiness to the greatest number, but let it become a system which provides the greatest unhappiness to the greatest number, and the world will come to an end.

What the people of the world want is the Four Freedoms, and no extensive controls are needed to give them those. Let those be their fundamental rights and let the people speak up when their rights are violated. But let us not drift into wanting to think for the people, act for the people, plan for the people. Those are the things the people should do for themselves.

For the Netherlands it is of special significance that a happy medium should be found between control and liberty. Although industry has increased in significance in the Netherlands in the last decades, commerce is of primary importance and will become even more so in the future. Holland's geographical position predestined it to be the gateway to Western Europe, and although the hinterland has changed considerably through the disintegration of Germany, it must not be overlooked that Germany, as an always threatening competitor, has been removed from the scene. Dutch ports may suffer from the small volume of trade with Germany, but they do not have to fear the competition of Hamburg and Bremen any longer. There are numerous new possibilities for Dutch commerce and industry which the government can aid but in which private initiative will have to be the deciding factor.

It does not have to be stressed that an expansion of Dutch commerce depends upon a speedy economic recovery of the country. The damage which was done can be distinguished as follows:

a)   damage to the productivity of labor.

b)   damage to the production capacity.

c)   losses in gold, foreign investment, etc.

When the war ended, the productive capacity of the Dutch worker had fallen considerably while this fact was aggravated by the lack of tools and machinery. According to estimates* labor productivity directly after the war had fallen to 40 per cent of the 1939 average while it is assumed, based on calculations made after the last war, that the former level will be reached again by the end of 1947.**

Decrease of production in the post-war period can be considered as war damage. Based upon the estimate of a decrease to 40 per cent with a gradual rise to 100 per cent by the end of 1947, we come to a loss due to the decrease of labor productivity of 85 per cent of normal annual production. As the annual production was around 5 billion guilders, this would mean a loss of 4.25 billion in 1939 money. Taking into account that prices have risen to about 175 per cent of the pre-war level, the actual loss in present money would amount to about 8 billion guilders.

The total value of the means of production, including soil, buildings, inventory and stock has been estimated*** at 26.6 billion guilders for September, 1939. The loss during the war years has been calculated at 7.7 billions or 29 per cent of the pre-war total. The damage consisted mainly of loss of fertility of the soil due to inundations and lack of fertilization, and damage to buildings and industrial equipment in Rotterdam as well as in the southern and eastern part of the country. Stocks and raw materials were confiscated on a vast scale, particularly toward the end of the war. Communications suffered a very severe loss: of a total of 1.5 billion in-

---

* In *de Schade en het herstel,* a study by J. J. van der Wal, I. van Ettinger, I. B. D. Derksen, L. T. Posthuma, A. de Graaf, J. van Luct, A. L. G. M. Rombouts.

** Labor productivity in November 1946 stood at 82 percent.

*** Cp. page 16 of the same publication.

vested in communications, 0.8 was destroyed. In detail the figures are as follows:

	Railroad	Shipping	Streetcars, Automobiles Busses
1939	0.4 billion	0.8 billion	0.3 billion
War Losses	0.2 "	0.3 "	0.3 "

The figure for the loss in streetcars, automobiles, etc., is undoubtedly exaggerated and 0.2 billion would be nearer the truth.

Thus, considering all factors, there was a decrease in production equipment from 26.6 billion to 18.9 billion. On the basis of the present prices, however, the latter figure would stand at 33 billion.

Financially there has been a tremendous increase in the national debt as well as in the money circulation. The national debt in January, 1940, amounted to about 4 billion guilders, 3,141 million consolidated and 825 million floating debt. On January 1, 1945, this amount had risen to 12 billion.

Next to this visible debt, there are the claims for war damages against the government which amount to about 2.5 billion guilders. Altogether the debt on May 1, 1945, consisted of about 15.5 billion guilders, meaning an increase of 11.5 billion guilders. The claims of 4.5 billion guilders which the Netherlands Bank has on Germany can be considered practically worthless.

If we add the figures for war damages on this basis, we arrive at the following result:

Loss caused by decreased labor productivity	4.25 billion
Loss of means of production	7.70 "
Loss of investments	2.80 "
TOTAL	14.75 "

The amount of 14.75 billion is according to the price level of 1939 and would be around 25 billions according to the prices of 1945. On this same basis the national wealth which was estimated at 33.3 billions in 1939 stands at 45.3 billions today but in this latter figure a rise in prices of 175 per cent is hidden.

The first point on which opinion in the Netherlands was practically unanimous was that inflation had to be stopped at all cost. When the enemy left Holland in May, 1945, note circulation stood at over 5½ billion guilders, as compared with 1,158 millions in May, 1940. In addition, bank balances amounted to between 4 and 6 billion guilders. There is no need to point out that, with the tremendous scarcity of goods, money circulation was entirely out of gear.

The Finance Minister of the Liberation Cabinet, Pieter Lieftinck, lost no time in working out a plan for a full-fledged restoration in order to create an equilibrium between money and goods. This was necessary in order to curb the black market, as well as to get a clear picture of the financial condition of the country.

The purge started on September 26, 1945, when all currency (bank notes and treasury notes) was withdrawn. At the same time, all balances with banks, savings banks, etc., were frozen. For one week, viz. September 26th-October 3rd, the flow of currency was stopped almost entirely. Against delivery of old notes (to be credited to current account of the depositor) each individual received 10 guilders (about $3.80) in new notes which was considered sufficient for the purchase of rationed foods. In that same period the withdrawal of old notes was completed. Silver and the new "zinc" coins were the only tender to remain in circulation. This difficult week, although it brought many complications to the population, was accepted with good humor.

On October 3rd, the second phase of the financial purge

began, namely, the gradual and limited deblocking for the payment of wages, salaries, pensions, etc.

On November 11, the new circulation amounted to 397 million guilders. After completion of the first stage of unfreezing, a gradual decrease of the rate of deblocking started until every enterprise was in a position to pay wages, salaries and stock purchases out of sales proceeds. The administrative measures connected with the unfreezing process have been complicated and sometimes cumbersome, but, on the whole they were carried out efficiently and fairly. There is no doubt, that the purge which was publicized widely all over the world was successful: at the end of 1945 banknote circulation stood at 1,386,000,000 guilders.

The results of such a purge are partly practical and partly psychological. The restoration of public confidence in the national money is the major factor while the freezing of a considerable amount of "floating purchasing power" tended to curb black market activities.

Blocked accounts are still somewhere between 3 and 4 billion guilders and can be used for such purposes as the payment of old taxes, payment of special levies, subscriptions to certain government loans, certain life insurance payments, etc.

It is amazing that few technical difficulties developed during the purge. The banks had to cope with hundreds of new small clients but apparently did so with success. There is also no doubt that black market activities have been strongly curtailed although this evil cannot be wiped out as long as there is a shortage of goods and price control has to be maintained.

As economic activity has increased steadily and with a price and wage level about 50 to 100 per cent higher than pre-war, note circulation has risen continuously and reached a level of about $2\frac{1}{2}$ billion guilders with minor fluctuations. In addition, free bank balances amount to about the same.

It is expected that the national income for 1946 will rise to 8.4 billion, as compared with 5 billion prior to the war, due to increased business activity and a higher price level. Modern economists have expressed the view that a money circulation (bank notes and free bank balances) of 50 per cent of the national income is an acceptable ratio so that the Netherlands seems to be on the right road.

Undoubtely there is still inflationary pressure but it is not excessive, and the constant control of the money supply as well as the increase in production seem to indicate that the trend is toward a sound situation.

Recently the Dutch government published details of a master plan for attaining national prosperity. It foresees speedy rehabilitation of key industries, a ceiling on domestic price rises, a vigorous export drive and further belt tightening by the government and the people.

The plan sets up a series of goals for 1946; building up production to 80 per cent of 1938, keeping the price level down to 185 per cent of that year, stepping up exports to a billion guilders and holding down imports to 2.8 billions.

Dutch production for the current year, as has been mentioned above, is estimated at 8.4 billion compared with less than 5 billion in 1938. In goods production this is about 80 percent of the 1938 figures.

Liquidation of floating foreign assets may yield 600 million guilders, including 120 million dollars and 30 million pounds sterling. In addition to this, foreign credits are necessary to the amount of 1,200 million guilders. At present the credit requirements are:

170 million dollars from the Import Export Bank.
15 million pounds from the Royal Dutch Shell.
A loan of 15 million pounds for military expenditures.
60 million dollars from Canada.
88 million guilders from other countries.

In addition to this, liquidation of 60 million dollars in American securities may prove necessary.

The national prosperity plan estimates government expenditures compared with 1938 as follows (in millions of guilders):

	CURRENT	1938
Wages and Salaries....................	1,235	405
Interest on pre-war loans..............	194	197
Materials	1,609	476
Interest on Wartime and Post-war loans, plus subsidiaries, etc.	1,240	414
TOTAL	4,278	1,492

Consumption at present is estimated at 74 per cent of 1938 or at present prices, between 6,700 and 7,460 million guilders.

The plan puts building requirements for 1946 at 790 millions of which 170 millions are considered new investments, including the cost of 10,000 houses to be completed before the year's end. Under expenditures for transport, 8,000 freight cars from the West European pool, plus repairs, will require 20 millions and 11,000 trucks, 5,000 automobiles and 24,000 busses will need 141 millions. The 850,000 gross tons of merchant shipping, or two thirds of war losses which will be partly built domestically and partly imported, is estimated at 200 million because, of the imported vessels, only 25 per cent will be paid in cash.

Repair of inland navigation will need 15 millions and capital requirements of K.L.M., the Royal Dutch Airlines, another 15 million.

Repair of the metal industry will need 350 millions, and other installations to be repaired over three years will need 550 millions this year. In addition, replacement of investments is calculated at 620 millions.

The total required for new investments, at 1946 prices, is estimated at 2 billion.

The plan sets forth the following budget (in billion guilders):

Net value of production	8.3	Consumption (excluding indirect taxes)	5.2
German reparations	0.1	Investments	2.0
Import balance	1.8	Government services	3.0
TOTAL	10.2	TOTAL	10.2

According to the reconstruction plan, rehabilitation of the metal industry is of primary importance, and therefore must be effected within a year, while full restoration of other industries, transport and agriculture are expected to be completed within three years and the building plan within 10 years.

Without foreign credits the prosperity level in 1947 will reach 50 per cent and with foreign credits of one billion guilders, 70 per cent of 1938 could be reached. Out of a national income of 8.6 billion, 1.1 billion should be saved, if necessary, by forced savings. The plan urges prohibition of the sale of or borrowing against non-liquid assets, unless exchanged for other non-liquid assets. It also recommends introduction of a rent tax to provide funds to subsidize new buildings.

The note rejects the idea of increasing foreign credits or extending liquidation of foreign assets beyond the contemplated sums, saying such action would only increase future burdens. It also rejects an increase in the guilder rate on the grounds that this would hamper exports.

The increase of coal production is of the greatest importance. At present it stands at 118,500 tons daily but should be raised to 125,400 tons in order to cover the urgent need.*

According to the author of the plan, Professor J. Tinbergen, head of the Central Planning Bureau, it remains a major handicap that the productivity of labor is still low and has not reached the 80 per cent of the pre-war level which was envisaged for 1946.

Government control of capital investment will have to remain in force in the Netherlands until private savings reach a volume sufficient to cover all government and other investment needs. Ultimately, all government controls of invest-

---

* In November 1946 daily production amounted to 31,000 tons.

ment will be abolished but this may require considerable time. The frozen money still represents an inflationary threat and unfreezing would lead to chaotic conditions.

In order to aid Holland's reconstruction, annexation of German territory has been suggested in many quarters. There has been a suitable flood of publications on this topic, with the pros outweighing the cons to a considerable extent. The annexation of German territory with the German population has found little support, but immediately after the war, a considerable clamor was raised for annexation of adjacent parts of Germany with removal of the inhabitants.

The economic arguments presented were that Holland needs more industries in order to offset her losses in income from foreign investments, shipping, overseas trading, etc., and that the annexation of German industrial territory might help to bring these changes about. However, lately the subject has become somewhat academic as there has already been so much shifting of Germany's population that one cannot visualize at the moment that any further forced removal of population would find much international support.*

The Netherlands' economy needs structural changes, but they will have to develop gradually, out of growing contacts with other countries. There is considerable room for commercial expansion for a nation as industrious, thrifty and level-headed as the Dutch and private enterprise will certainly find the best possible outlets, with the assistance of government, according to the method of trial and error. There are no big possibilities, but slowly and painstakingly more has been built in this world than according to preconceived schemes. As the inherent qualities of the Dutch have not changed through this war, there is no reason to doubt that they again will find a solution for their problems as they have done for twenty centuries.

---

* Recently the Netherlands government has presented claims for minor border rectifications.

CHAPTER VII

Reconstruction Applied

IN THE RECONSTRUCTION of war shattered areas there are two major factors involved: The men and the tools. To obtain the necessary tools, the combined efforts of nations or, at any rate, large groups are necessary; the human factor without the proper tools seems rather ineffective nowadays and yet it furnishes the spark which sets the engine going.

Our modern machines are the work of people who had arduous tasks to perform, and who gradually discovered means which enabled them to enlist the help of hitherto unutilized natural forces. However, the will to perform these tasks was first and without the sweat and blood used on them, no inventions would have been made. Emergencies and the will to solve them were the underlying causes which enabled mankind to perform its great achievements. Once the modern means are in existence, it is a normal procedure to wait for them and to apply no more energy than is really needed. Yet, there is a danger in this idea of a properly balanced attitude as it may ultimately make us forget these supreme efforts which keep the wheels of history turning. A balanced world is one which carries the ultimate seeds of deterioration although it may take a long time before they reach the surface. When Plato described his perfect state, he remarked that somehow even in the perfect state, the roots of decay are present. The laws of nature remain unchanged, and only the use of all human faculties, talents and capacities will maintain human energy on the level which the mastery of life demands.

Stoicism as the aftermath of hedonism may ultimately prove a form of life which freezes too many of our capabilities. Perhaps this explains why there is something refreshing and awe-inspiring about people who tackle a major job with nothing more than a lot of spirit and their hands to help them.

It signifies the same directness of approach which pioneers and adventurers possess: the perhaps unwise decision to ignore the rest of the world and to shape things the way we want them. It may not be the way we visualize the world of the future, but it has the human appeal which anything too premeditated, too well calculated, lacks.

The breath of originality has become so rare that every time it is noticeable it deserves fanfares and trumpets, especially if it takes the form of a certain disdain for progress and all its facilities. A disdain not dictated by the boredom of too many facilities, but by hard necessity and a strong will.

The story of the isle of Walcheren is a vivid example of all this. It is, in reality, a simple story which should be simply told. The people who were in it probably did not feel heroic about it but just determined in a business-like way.

When Walcheren was liberated in November, 1944, five-sixths of its territory was flooded. West of the canal Flushing-Middelburg-Veere about 31 thousand acres were flooded, while there was an additional area of about 5,000 acres south of Flushing. The dike along the canal separated the two flooded areas which surrounded the badly damaged historic city of Middelburg.

The northeastern, northwestern and southwestern parts of the island were under water except for the dunes along the coast and the higher centers of some of the villages. Four gaps in the dikes surrounding the island had given Walcheren back to the ocean: one gap of 270 yards, northwest of Flushing, called "De Nolle"; another gap of 435 yards near Westkapelle on the north shore of the island; northwest of Veere an additional three gaps of about 765 yards width altogether.

These three were interconnected which created a number of complicated problems in regard to the closing of the dikes.

Near Flushing there were a few smaller breaches, but a major problem was created by the opening near Fort Rammekens which was 810 yards wide and surrounded by mine fields.

The island looked pretty hopeless, with only one item on the positive side of the ledger: considerable quantities of food left by the Germans made it easier to look after the population which stuck tenaciously to its beloved island. However, there was little to report otherwise except water everywhere: no electricity, no gas, destroyed locks, no water, no functioning pumping installations, mines and more mines. There was practically no material available for the closing of the gaps—and lots of it was necessary: suction pumps and pressure pumps, miles of pipes, tugboats, digging equipment, millions of bundles of osiers, stones to add weight to the frames of osiers to be sunk in the gaps, and a million other things like housing, food, and equipment for thousands of workers. None of these things except a few thousand tons of stone were to be found on Walcheren.

No wonder the outsiders who looked at the raging masses of water with the destroyed villages rising dismally above this expanse of grey desolation were in favor of giving up and leaving the small area in the possession of a victorious ocean.

The Dutch who may have had a mental picture of their whole country once looking pretty much the same way, never even considered the question.

"When will Walcheren be dry?" was the only question they asked themselves.

The Department of Waterworks lost no time in sending down one of the ablest engineers, P. Ph. Jansen, who surveyed matters and decided that they were urgent. The possibility of giving Walcheren up he didn't deign worth mention.

Every day the gaps were becoming larger and deeper, and the ocean, according to its mood, would conquer additional slices of land. There was no time to be lost and the section Reclamation of Walcheren, officially installed, began to tackle its task with speed and determination.

It is hard to imagine now how primitive conditions were. No offices, no typewriters, no drafting boards, no pencils. Only problems. Make-shift offices had to be installed in halfway usable houses; garages were made of the vegetable market, a dancing pavillion was transformed into living quarters for the workers, etc. Individual ingenuity had to find a solution for everything.

German barracks were collected wherever they could be found, even if they stood in a mine field. Bunkers in the dunes provided additional living quarters as well as "Nissen Shelters" which the allies donated. Generous Switzerland came across with spick and span barracks for 2,000 men and thus, in one way or another, the men who were to do the job could at least live on Walcheren Island.

During the icy winter, the men doing the electrical work moved over the island in row boats and repaired the cables so that by the spring, there was light again everywhere on the island.

But, during the winter and early spring, the war was still raging and Europe, as well as the Netherlands, had graver problems than the reclamation of Walcheren. All the engineers could do was to keep the gaps as small as possible and partly repair the havoc which every new storm created. The regions where the osiers are found were still in German hands, the stones were in Belgium where they were needed for repairs on the Allied airfields, and all the engineers could do was to wait and make soundings and drawings.

Some material arrives, some goes to the bottom of the sea or is shelled by the Germans. And to many of the workers it seems that there is nothing much but mines in this world.

The Belgians give considerable aid: Their suction pumps, a dredger, miles of pipe and narrow gage railroad equipment. Also stones and osiers begin to arrive but still in small quantities.

Finally on May 8th, 1945, the liberation of the tortured northern Netherlands came, but there was no time for jubilation in Walcheren. Hurried messages were sent north for tugboats, dredges and cranes and all the other equipment of which Walcheren had only small quantities.

In the beginning, the Department of Waterworks had kept the reclamation of Walcheren under its own auspices, but later on it decided to follow the same procedure which was used in the case of the Zuiderzee works, viz., to give it to a combination of contractors on a cost and profit basis. This was the quickest way to get things done, a method which was also followed in the United States for war contracts. As circumstances did not permit an accurate calculation, the costs could not be determined in advance.

A somewhat unusual procedure was followed, namely, that the Department had to approve all expenditures and kept the ultimate control, while the contractors carried out the work. It was an unorthodox method which has been criticized, but it was obviously the only possible way under the prevailing circumstances. It was stipulated by the government that firms which had shown a collaborationist attitude during the war could not form part of the combine.

An unexpected hitch developed when it proved difficult to find workers. The Walcheren combine offered 52 cents an hour while the Allies in Brabant offered 75 cents. The workers, even when they got higher wages, remained displeased because the money did not buy them anything. They put in understandable demands for shirts, overalls, shoes, raincoats and tobacco.

The psychological exhaustion which was noticeable everywhere in the Netherlands did not leave Walcheren untouched.

The dikeworkers came from the region of the large rivers, from Werkendam and Sliedrecht, old villages crouching beneath the dikes, from which they set out to build dams in all parts of the world. They have strong arms and strong principles. Working on Sundays was against their traditions and their Christian beliefs, and it took a long time before they could see that the emergency on Walcheren over-ruled all principles.

However, things kept moving at a varied pace although the visitor to Walcheren would see little change in the scene of desolation. At high tide—the difference between the tides at times amounts to 13 yards—destroyed roofs and damaged church spires would be the only visible things while at low tide, the houses overgrown with mussels and seaweed would present a weird picture. Once the greenest spot in colorful Holland, Walcheren had turned a dismal, sandish grey, an uninterrupted plain which had no sign of life except the slowly circling seagulls. Without the aid of the British Ducks, life would have come to an end in Walcheren, but the helpful English Allies kept up the so badly needed communications. They were able to reach the villages built on mounds where the inhabitants tried to continue life as well as possible.

No force on earth would have made them leave, and even those whose houses were flooded to the top floor needed a lot of persuasion before they climbed down from their roofs. How these people managed to be in immaculate native costumes is such a typically Dutch secret that it cannot be divulged.

Praying and hoping was their way of regaining their island as well as hard physical labor on the dikes, but they had no patience for the intricacies of modern engineering.

Westkapelle, where the first landing was made in a bloody and hard-fought battle, was the first place where the defense against the sea was turned into a major, well-planned attack. The charming village was completely flattened by the furious fighting, and along its famous dike one sees nothing but bunkers and twisted and broken gun emplacements. German prisoners, ignored by everybody, were around to clear their own mines away. They presented a sad picture and must have been aware of the cold contempt which the inhabitants showed them.

Shelters and barracks house the workers while there is a canteen which provides beer. The more badly wanted gin is not around, to the dismay of those who stand in the cold sea water for the major part of the day. The canteen is decorated with excellent cartoons, and once a week entertainers come up from Amsterdam or The Hague to cheer the workers. Sturdy and pretty Zeeland girls serve the men their beer which still leaves a nostalgia for pre-war days.

The scene of reconstruction seems utterly disconnected to the layman. But let us first describe its initial stages. To repair a broken dike one does not start on the old one, but a new dike is constructed farther inland. There are several reasons for this: The low tide draws deep furrows in the soil which would be hard to fill while work on the old dike would have to take place in the open ocean, mostly a rather unruly place. By building a dike farther inland first, the work can take place in the little inland harbor which the water has created. In this little harbor it is quiet and the dredges and landing boats can do their work.

Behind the original dike there is a sort of oblong, picturesque pond of greatly varying depth which ultimately will be landscaped and provide ideal bathing and canoeing. On its sides the inland dike arises as tenacles which slowly reach across. They are made partly by hand, partly by dredges and huge pressure pumps which transport a mixture of sand and water. The water drains off, the sand remains, although it seems a slow process when one watches it. Then a defense is built on the outside of the provisional dam: it gets a coat of heavy clay and on this coat a sort of wicker work of willows or osiers is placed. Then, heavier poles are driven into this framework, and willow twigs are woven along these poles in a way which reminds one of knitting.

But it is a way of knitting which requires a lot of skill and which is the result of centuries of experience. Only special workers can do this, and the knowledge of the value of their work for Holland has made them into a proud, strong and stubborn race.

On this solid framework stones are placed which the branches keep in place so that the beating waves exhaust themselves in fruitless attacks. Whenever the dike gets to the places where the water has made deep gullies, "Zink-stukken" are dropped. These "sink pieces" resemble big wafers made of willows which are woven in an artful way. They are the alpha and omega of dike building and furnish the foundation upon which the dike rests. They are about 32 yards long, and when ready they present a neat picture of little squares of willow twigs surrounded by heavier branches. Ultimately, all the cross-points are tied together and on the basic frame three rows of willow bundles are placed while they are topped once more by a framework similar to the basic one.

Then a lower and upper frame are tied together, and we have a solid tremendous "wafer" made of willows which will float on the water in the proper place until quantities of heavy stones are dropped on them and make them sink to form the foundation of the dike to come.

The placing of the "sink piece" and the proper moment of sinking is a matter of great skill which involves tides, wind velocity and numerous other factors. Its secret of success lies in its elasticity because, if it were stiff, the water would draw gullies underneath. It adjusts itself, however, to the uneven-ness of the soil and presents a solid front to the attacking water.

Another complication is furnished by the fact that a "sink piece" cannot be brought to its place by tugboat. The swell of the tugboat would damage it easily so that the "sink piece" is attached to a big, flat bottomed boat which is pulled in turn by a tugboat. If one watches this work, one feels the excitement of a complicated operation when everyone holds his breath at the critical moment. Weeks of work can be spoiled by a wrong move. When the sink piece is finally in the proper spot—and this is a matter of inches—it is anchored swiftly by the quickest boys of the crew. It is also secured from the shore with heavy hawsers, and then everybody hopes that it will stay in its place. It is brought there during high tide so that it floats in with the current, but it has to be anchored also from the other side in view of the turning tide.

Then, tons of stone are dropped on it neatly and systematically and, at a given moment, the hawsers are disconnected and the "sink piece" disappears to the bottom to form the foundation of the dike. All these activities proceed pretty regularly for the most part until the breach in the dike becomes narrower and narrower, and, consequently, the current becomes stronger and stronger.

Then, the undertaking begins to take on dramatic aspects: a fullfledged battle between the sea and the ingenuity of man. Particularly strenuous and drawnout was the battle for the "Nollegat" which was closed successfully at first only to succumb once more to the furious onslaughts of the northwestern storms.

In the beginning of June, 1945, the gap between the two dams at the Nolle was about 360 yards wide. During the periods of dead tide the dikes were extended as rapidly as possible, but storms widened the gap again on several occasions. As the progress was slow, all available equipment was mobilized and a huge crane started to drop heavy clay, which had to come from another part of Holland, into the gap.

But even these measures were upset by the stormy month of August so that ultimately, floating caissons which the British used during the invasion were sunk in the gap. When there were only thirty more yards to go, a violent storm smashed caissons, cranes and whatever else there was to destroy, and once more the gap widened to over seventy yards.

Success was finally achieved when the engineers sank German landing-boats and used torpedo nets to break the current in the remaining gap. The use of the torpedo nets for this purpose was entirely a stroke of genius as nobody had ever thought of this before. Finally, in the first days of September, the gap was closed but the victory proved to be only temporary.

In the second half of September after a period of strong western and southwestern storms, the wind suddenly shifted to the north. The Channel was too narrow to digest the masses of water, and on September 19 the high tide swept swiftly and devastatingly over the new dam taking its top away. No immediate aid was feasible, and soon, on September 25, the new dam collapsed and the sea rolled into that section of Walcheren island once more. Swiftly the new breach widened, and everything that had been used to fill it was swept away into unknown depths.

All efforts to halt the disaster were in vain. The weather remained rough and even the most skilled engineers felt that they were waging a hopeless battle. As small caissons disappeared as quickly as they were placed, a major campaign was launched with one forty yards long and 18 yards wide. Torpedo nets galore were dropped on top while the British supplied the dynamite and men to handle it.

Additional caissons, additional torpedo nets, and tons of clay finally did the trick, and this time Walcheren was really saved in the nick of time. On the night of October 2, 1945, at 10 minutes to three, the last yards were conquered and the most serious menace to Walcheren ceased to exist.

There was not the same amount of drama about the closing of the other gaps although they all presented their own specific problems. At Westkapelle the open ocean and its treacherous breakers presented a major problem as it continuously threatened to throw the heavy equipment right on the land. If the weather did not interfere, the work at Westkapelle progressed steadily and the dams on both sides neared one another with regularity. Toward the end, caissons were sunk and stone breakers were built beyond the projected dam to break the waves which, at times, would nibble away parts of the dam, and, naturally, became more menacing as the gap narrowed.

As the Westkapelle dike has a bend at the place where the breach occurred, the strongest currents and counter-currents occurred, and behind the dike there is a new lake of irregular formation which reaches considerable depth in spots.

When the breach narrowed, the same procedure was followed as at "De Nolle": concrete caissons were sunk of which many disappeared in foul weather, but finally two larger ones were successfully placed. As many caissons, sandboats and cranes had been wrecked, it required quite some seamanship toward the end to bring anything to the proper spot. Lots of clay, sand, and, once more, the torpedo nets, took care of the remaining rifts, and again the ocean had to admit defeat.

In the minds of the inhabitants of Westkapelle, their village must have looked pretty and peaceful again, and beyond the ruins they saw a green island emerging from the waves, perhaps an even more beautiful island than they had known in the past.

The breach at Veere was closed more quickly than anticipated as the forecasts from the Bureau of Hydraulic Engineering at Delft were unfavorable for closing in the second half of October as had been planned at first. In five days and nights of furious work, the gap near the forlorn, out-of-the-world city of Veere was filled in much the same way as the others.

And then the miracle occurred: the water began to flow out of Walcheren, the water that had invaded the island for 13 months began to withdraw and to flow back into the river Schelde and the sea when the locks were opened. A special outlet to the Middelburg-Veere Canal was made to speed the process of natural drainage and the locks were opened to let the accumulated water masses out. The surging of the retreating water must have been music to the ears of those who had seen it flow in and out of the island four times a day with the turning tides. And now it had become one-way traffic with no return for Holland's traditional enemy.

The remaining flooded region near Middelburg was a unit in itself and did not prevent the drainage of the major part of the island.

When the author came to Walcheren in December, 1945, no more violent battles against the water were raging except near Fort Rammekens. The tremendous success which had been achieved was not immediately visible to the outsider. The island still looked forlorn and desolate while a primitive life was carried on in the battered villages. Occasionally somebody would be puttering at a house still overgrown with seaweed and mussels.

The roads reminded one of the sandy trails in Africa, with only occasional stretches where the pavement was intact. The bunkers in the dunes had been converted into friendly looking homes with flowers and curtains. The ugly signs "Mines" were still frequent and the Germans had added an additional touch of desolation by placing poles all over the island in order to prevent parachute landings.

At Westkapelle the major dike was being rebuilt gradually although there was a shortage of the type of stone which is generally used for this work. Other parts of the formidable sea dike badly needed repairs as the battle against the sea is a continuous one.

There was comfort in the heavy steady work of hundreds of men laboring quietly or singing their traditional ballads of love, of beautiful girls and wicked men.

The sea lends an aspect of eternity and dignity to this type of work which never ends and exemplifies our constant struggle with nature in one of its most primitive forms. The huge dredges looked tiny bobbing up and down on the breakers or waiting farther out for a change in tide.

I had the feeling that the war had not changed Holland much; that this had gone on for centuries and would continue to for many more centuries to come. The few German prisoners in their uniforms looked rather ridiculous against this background of majestic, quiet work as if they were shrinking away, contemplating their own evil ambitions.

"The breakers sing in never ending murmurs," as one of Holland's poets once said. To fill the nostalgia of years of absence completely, huge white clouds—clouds as only Holland has—drifted slowly across a deep blue sky. I had no difficulty in understanding the deep love of these people for their land with its great beauty and the spirit of seclusion and intimacy. I could understand how impatiently they had watched the work on the dikes, waiting for the moment which must have meant everything to them. And now, with quiet, unspoken satisfaction, they moved about in their shattered villages, repairing whatever could be repaired.

The last gap at Fort Rammekens still gave a good idea of how things had been everywhere some time before.

After we arrived there over a narrow dike running across muddy water, I was given a pair of big rubber boots so that I would be able to cope with the situation. Unfortunately, they were a few sizes too large, and with every step I took, they showed a strong tendency to stay behind in the heavy clay and to let me walk on alone. As I was not prepared for this—there was no chapter about this emergency in the book,

How to Behave Under Unforseen Circumstances—I landed practically flat on my face with the first step I took.

The dike workers watched my struggle with grave concern, but I had a suspicion that they would have let out the dike workers' yell if the mud had proved victorious. However, at the cost of much perspiration, the boots and I gradually made our way to a little tugboat which was going to take us to the gap in the dike. It was one of the strangest trips I ever took: sometimes it was like shooting the rapids, then it would be like floating around on a miniature polar sea with mountains of white foam representing the icebergs, and then, nearing the open sea, we ran quietly aground hoping there were no mines in the neighborhood.

The waters turned and whirled around us as if we were on the "Maid of the Mist" while there were dozens of small Niagara Falls all around us. A sudden switch in one of the currents pulled us free again, and we proceeded slowly through this strangest of all landscapes.

Our adventures in Walcheren were very minor compared to those other people went through. When Walcheren is once more a well-regulated island where people lead normal, peaceful lives, some tall tales will be spun around the period of reclamation, and if this were a different century, it would become the source of long and romantic ballads. War, water and wind is a dramatic combination of which only Walcheren can claim to have been the scene. There is room for a great epic about its heroic story.

CHAPTER VIII

Holland's Place in the World

O N OUR CIRCLING globe the Dutch appear in quite a few places, but it fills them with only moderate pride —or a moderate inferiority complex, depending on how the barometer reads—as they can still think of the days when they were a leading world power. In the bizarre and colorful world of the sixteenth and seventeenth centuries they roamed all over the earth, monopolized a good deal of shipping and trade, and at the same time produced a few religions, philosophies, paintings, compositions, etc., of considerable merit while their architecture created cities which can still claim an unsurpassed beauty all their own. Then, in the eighteenth century, the tide turned, and Holland slept in smug enjoyment of its own excellence without adding much to it.

In the second half of the eighteenth century there was another upsurge of the Dutch spirit although it remained far behind that of its Golden Age. Liberalism, as a renewal of the Humanism of the past, created a strong interest in improved colonial administration, in more democracy in the home country, in commerce and industry as well as in literature and the exact sciences. There was also a mild renaissance in painting, but it did not produce great geniuses except Van Gogh who found the atmosphere of Holland rather stifling and spent most of his life in France.

The twentieth century saw a continuation of these trends: there was much of the *"bourgeois satisfait"* attitude, a good deal of energetic work, a considerable amount of hypocrisy and mutual adoration, and some remarkable peaks of achievement in the exact sciences, engineering and architecture.

Literature began to be more and more a highbrow affair which was strictly for the "refined classes," and little of it penetrated across the national border except lyrical poetry which took a sudden upswing, possibly as a revolt against overly-conscious intellectualism and the regimented mentality of a bourgeois civilization.

The modern Dutchman of means and talent was rapidly becoming very international: a high standard of living permitted him to live or study in other countries, and the number of people of independent means had become quite considerable. They furnished welcome trialgrounds for experiments in philosophy, education, art or whatever else might occupy their fancies. As there was no outspoken leisure class in Holland which busied itself merely with social activities—this being against the Puritan traditions of the country—everybody pursued some interest which bred an atmosphere of culture and well being, similar to that of the other western European countries, but on a broader material basis.

It is no wonder, therefore, that Holland had excellent orchestras, beautiful homes and public buildings, excellent universities and schools, interesting literature, good painting, and sufficient outlets for those who sought more exciting lives in the overseas territories or other parts of the world.

There was still something of the spirit of the "seigneur" about Holland, of the patricians of birth and wealth who looked down from their well-furnished homes on the rest of the population which took its revenge in occasional Breughelesque outbursts of not always tasteful gaiety. Wealth was more unevenly distributed than, for instance, in Switzerland and Norway as there were some very rich families and a considerable number of very poor ones. In its social stratification, Holland has some of the attributes of a larger country, perhaps because its overseas territories prevented its upper classes from becoming provincial. Dutch captains of commerce or industry are hard-headed but willing to admit achievement except perhaps in the realm of medium and small enterprises where nepotism rules to a very extensive degree, probably somewhat to the detriment of the country although it gives a certain stability to its social structure. The Dutchman at home is generally rather stiff and well-behaved but when he crosses the border, he feels sometimes the necessity of showing a lighter spirit or of reverting to the somewhat boisterous pleasures of his ancestors. The "haves" and "have nots," the believers and the unbelievers, the conservatives and the progressives blend in numerous variations, and, in general, people's attitudes are limited for the most part by the nearness of their neighbors.

Most Dutchmen will praise their country, but add immediately: "It is becoming so small that I like to get out of it."

Small it has become indeed: a car takes one all over Holland, from north to south and from east to west, in a single day, and everywhere there are towns and villages, and everywhere people, except for a few forest regions where the winter brings peace and quiet. Yet, there are still considerable regional differences, but how long they will maintain themselves is open to conjecture.

It is natural that the presence of many people on a small territory fills many with anxiety about the future. The war has strongly aggravated this concern, and at the moment, it is perhaps the problem which is uppermost in the minds of most Dutchmen.

They realize that Holland has to reconsider its place in the world, and they are not definite in what way reorientation will be possible. A definite thread runs through the entire history of Holland: every time one continental European power became too strong, Holland's independence has been severely threatened. A balance of power in Europe has been the permanent condition of Holland's existence, and this fundamental principle, viz., the absence of a dominating power on the continent, has closely aligned it with Great

Britain ever since the beginnings of its independence for British policy has consistently pursued this aim over a period of several centuries.

The revolution of Holland against Spain has been too often depicted as an individual effort of the Netherlands of which the international aspects were not sufficiently realized. Spain was the first European nation which aimed at complete domination of the continent and which immediately generated the resistance of other powers to this effort.

Holland was the country where Spanish imperialism created strong opposition, but this was felt by no means as a purely Netherlands affair at that time. The Prince of Orange, in the beginning of the war against Spain, felt himself a prince of the Holy Roman Empire and looked toward the north-German states for aid in his struggle against the centralizing influence of Philip II of Spain. Only when these efforts failed did the Prince of Orange realize that help had to be found in other quarters and that the Netherlands had to rely mostly upon themselves. As soon as the Netherlands had gained their independence, their first concern has always been to see that no major power developed on its borders. Annexation has never been, and may still not be today, Dutch policy as Holland generally pursued a trend of negative interference of striving to be surrounded by weak neighbors. In the eighteenth and nineteenth centuries there was no danger from the eastern side as Germany was internally divided and showed too little unity to provide a threat to Dutch independence. Every time greater unity appeared on the horizon, the Dutch, by helping the towns against the princes, or one region against another, tried to prevent unification. Eastern Frisia was long considered a strategic region where the United Provinces maintained garrisons until the days of Frederick the Great.

England and France immediately realized the crucial significance of Dutch resistance against Spain, and gave Holland the valuable opportunity to seek aid from one or the other but also to balance them against one another. The balance of power has been the principle of Holland's creation as well as of its continued existence. It has always sought the support of another power as long as it did not threaten to become too strong.

In the beginning of the Eighty Years' War, leading statesmen like the Prince of Orange, The Grand Pensionary Bugs, and others did not think of complete sovereignty, but of a protectorate as the ultimate goal of their efforts. The sovereignty over Holland was offered on several occasions to Queen Elizabeth of England, but England was not interested in territory on the continent although it was willing to send Leicester as military commander and to aid the Dutch. France, also, was requested to accept a kind of protectorate over Holland on several occasions, but when these efforts came to naught, Dutch self-confidence and its dependence upon a balance of power gradually began to grow. When, in 1596, it was admitted into a Triple Alliance with England and France, it was certain of its existence as a free, independent sovereign state.

The position of England in regard to the Netherlands has always been of particular significance. "England cannot tolerate a major power on the other side of the North Sea. . . . It also is opposed to a weak power without resistance of its own because this would provide a temptation for occupation by a stronger power. Thus, history shows the two countries England and Holland in an unbroken inter-relationship. England was always for us when we were threatened, and against us when we were too powerful ourselves or overwhelmed by another power."*

These same principles were already valid in the time of Elizabeth when the Netherlands were regarded as one of

* Cf. Van Hamel, "Nederland Tusschen de Morgendheden," Amsterdam, 1918.

England's ramparts. England's interest was to support Holland, but to prevent it from becoming too strong so that its lines of behavior often seemed whimsical and illogical although they were controlled by the same guiding principle. For that same reason, England has never been interested in controlling the Netherlands territorially, but it has been quite eager to maintain garrisons in the Dutch ports which control the Channel. The Netherlands never conceded this point although Flushing and another city were given as "collateral" for financial assistance in the days of Leicester.

At the time that England's support was essential to the cause of the Netherlands, there were always groups in Holland which considered too close an association dangerous and which urged more intimate ties with France. The Anglophiles and the Francophiles were two definite parties which changed in importance in accordance with the problems of the moment.

The fact that England and France jealously watched each other's influence on Holland only tended to strengthen Holland's position. With the growing power of France, Holland became the link, but also the wall, between England and France which were both opposed to the aspirations of the Hapsburgs but were equally wary of one another. This determined the necessary line of Dutch diplomacy: to be the link between Great Britain and the second power on the continent in order to keep the dominating power in check. This function made Holland too valuable ever to be absorbed unless one power temporarily dominated the others as occurred three times in history. However, during the period of the Eighty Years' War, it was definitely Holland which manipulated these forces to its own advantage.

Both England and France were becoming concerned about the growing power of the republic in the beginning of the seventeenth century. It was more than they had bargained for. Holland's increasing maritime power was a thorn in

England's side while France did not like to see Holland grow into a strong continental power. Thus, both powers were eager to see the war with Spain continued, "to blow the coals of war, not to quench them," and it was a major triumph of Dutch diplomacy when, in 1609, a temporary peace with Spain was achieved, although it only lasted until 1618 when Holland was drawn into the maelstrom of the Thirty Years' War.

This war has been interpreted as the struggle of the progressive nations, striving for a Europe consisting of sovereign countries, against the reactionary and centralistic tendencies of the Hapsburgs. Sweden, with Gustavus Adolphus, France under Richelieu, and the Netherlands under the Oranges, fought the battle for the modernization of Europe which definitely weakened the Holy Roman Empire to the point of a nominal structure, and confirmed the balance of power as the system under which the sovereign states were to live for the coming centuries. Although the Treaty of Westphalia gave recognition to the Netherlands as an independent power, it was at this same time that France's increasing might posed a new problem for the Netherlands. Immediately after the Peace of Westphalia, the French, themselves, saw their role merely as keeping the imperial power in check by seeking friends among the smaller countries and by manipulating the divided and weakened German states. The breaking up of Germany into smaller states has been a constant aim of France. This aim was carried out by Napoleon I as well as by Napoleon III, and was pursued again after World War I and after World War II.

The position of Belgium as a possible gateway to France was of eternal concern to the French as well as to the Dutch who preferred France as a friend to France as a neighbor. This has always been the main reason why the Northern Netherlands never armed, except in isolated instances, in unison with the Southern Netherlands which would place

France at her southern borders. Therefore, the Netherlands has consistently attempted to keep control of the mouths of the rivers leading to the Southern Netherlands, but not to exercise any direct control. Security in the South was one of the main reasons for Holland's participation in the Thirty Years' War. It was Holland's aim to keep Belgium in existence as long as Spain was too weak to make it into a power of any consequence.

It is another instance of the "barrier system" whereby Holland tried to protect itself by attempting to be surrounded by weak states. Commercial considerations led to the same conclusions as the North was anxious to maintain its economic supremacy. Thus, in this case, the merchant and the statesman were in accord about their aims. The merchants were energetic supporters of the war party which was afraid of the competition of Flanders and Antwerp.

The Treaty of 1635 between the Netherlands and France aided France in its development toward a major power, but was soon viewed with concern by the Netherlands. Enthusiasm for unity with the Southern Netherlands died out completely, and the idea of an independent Belgian republic was also abandoned as Holland was not entirely displeased to keep Spain somewhere in the picture.

The Treaty of Westphalia defined the political philosophy of Europe for the future: the existence of sovereign states which were anxious to live in general and permanent peace. The idea of a general empire was definitely abandoned in favor of the principle of multiple sovereignty; attempts to have the Netherlands maintain some allegiance to the Empire came to naught.

In the relationship of the Netherlands with its neighbors, it became necessary in each case to determine at some time who was the stronger party. This problem became acute for the first time with England which aided Holland in gaining its freedom from Spain, but was exceedingly jealous of its commercial supremacy, especially in the overseas territories. It is remarkable that the first English war was preceded by an offer from Cromwell to unite the two powers into one body.

While England and Holland needed one another politically, they were commercial competitors which led to a strange relationship somewhat like a competition between two friends. In spite of the bitter wars which were fought to destroy Holland's supremacy on the seas, there remained a fundamental affinity between the two countries. While Holland was, without any doubt, the leading maritime power in the beginning of the seventeenth century, it lost this position in the second half and has since that time lost more of its power than was perhaps beneficial to the well-being of Europe.

As an insular power, England could never tolerate the domination of the seas by another power, and, as soon as they realized that the Dutch were heading that way, they systematically set about the task of gaining that power for themselves by impeding Duch trade and fisheries, culminating these efforts in the famous Navigation Act of 1609 and by fighting three consecutive sea wars against the Dutch which definitely established British supremacy in the end.

The Dutch were deeply disturbed about the interference with their commerce. Even at that time it was clearly realized that Holland, small and over-populated even in those days, needed commerce as the foundation of its existence more than any other nation.

Each time, however, when danger threatened on the continent, the more far-sighted leaders in England and Holland again became conscious of the common interests of the two nations, so that the seventeenth century presents the strange picture of periods of friendship as well as periods of bitter warfare. While Holland's influence declined in the North Seas, English writers at the end of the seventeenth century still had occasion to point to the successes in the Baltic and Russian seas, as well as in the Far East. The Dutch, themselves, resorted to war only in the case of utmost necessity. They regarded trade as their chief object in life and felt that the wars of others only added to their commercial opportunities while the wars themselves did not concern them although they were eager to act as promoters of peace, defenders of international law, and as advocates of the balance of power.

For a period in the middle of the seventeenth century, Holland kept itself aloof from all foreign alliances in order to promote its commerce as much as possible, but the far-reaching plans of expansion of Louis XIV made it enter an alliance with England and Sweden in 1660.

The treaty came too late to stop the ambitions of France which De Witt had insufficiently realized while the rest of the nation had been too thoroughly absorbed in commerce to observe the signs of the approaching storm.

At the last moment when Holland's cause seemed almost lost, Stadholder William III, by an energetic diplomatic and military policy, succeeded in turning the tide and in making the European powers realize the danger of French imperialism. It was to a large degree due to William's merit that the European nations formed a coalition against France.

The marriage of William III to Princess Mary of England aided in bringing about the so vitally needed collaboration between Holland and England. However, in spite of William's determination, the Netherlands did not regain their power as fully as possible due to the pacifistic, materialistic attitude of the regents which followed again a short-sighted policy as soon as the worst danger had been averted. The French very cleverly played on the fear of the Dutch merchants of English competition, and especially in Amsterdam, a Francophile attitude began to prevail which became a factor in shortening a war which might have brought decisive defeat to France. When the war came to an end in 1678, it had become eminently clear, however, that the Netherlands was a major factor in maintaining the balance of power: it was the axle around which European politics revolved. A statue on the Dôme des Invalides in Paris clearly expresses that France, at that time, regarded Holland as the most formidable of her opponents.

The growing power of France was hardly curbed by the Peace of 1678, and William III remained one of the few who were completely aware of the French plans for the revival of the Hapsburg Empire, this time under the leadership of the Bourbons. France annexed territories in a subtle way and, at the same time, proclaimed herself as the defender of international law and world peace, although she interpreted these concepts much to her own liking.

If, at that time, William III—as king of England—had not been able to mobilize England's strength, French supremacy might have been definitely established on the continent. Although William III finally achieved the close coalition with England of which Cromwell had dreamt, even he was not able to remove discrimination against Dutch shipping and Dutch commercial interests.

The firm alliance between England and Holland, together with a number of other powers, was continued after the death of William III until the Peace of Utrecht which reestablished the balance of power on the European continent for almost a century.

Van Hamel, in his excellent work, *Nederland Tusschen de Mogendheden,* points out how Holland has aided the establishment of English power in the same way that it assisted in the growth of France after the Treaty of Westphalia.

The Peace of Utrecht reconfirmed Holland's position as a European power although it probably could have bettered its conditions if it had made less excessive demands in regard to Belgium. The necessity of a barrier system to protect Holland from its powerful neighbors was fully acknowledged so that the Netherlands felt that it was built upon a firm and stable foundation which would not be subjected to attacks by other nations in the future.

After the Peace of Utrecht, Dutch policy became self-satisfied, less alert and has little to record except short-sightedness and complacency. The regents with their eternal policy of caution and procrastination did much to sap the lifeblood of the nation. In the period after 1702, Holland demonstrated clearly that a foreign policy dominated by purely commercial considerations only leads to weakness against powers which are willing to risk more than profits or losses. Holland believed more in international peace than observation of reality warranted, because it considered these trends favorable to its business interests. It was a situation which, in some respects, reminds one of the period preceding World War II, although, when put to the test, the nation showed amazing vitality and its attitude could in no way be compared to the weakness of the French period.

Yet, among leading circles there was in 1940 perhaps too much faith in the validity of international law and international agreements.

The eighteenth century was a period in which there was continuous talk of perpetual peace and international organization, but these concepts were used selfishly by the more astute powers which would not have dreamt of renouncing a particle of their sovereignty. On the contrary, it was the idea of sovereignty which dominated European political thinking in the eighteenth, nineteenth and first decades of the twentieth century although there were rumblings in the more distant future which, as yet, had no validity in the official world.

Holland's belief in internationalism at such an early period could be construed, posthumously, as farsightedness, but such an elegant solution would hardly do justice to a period which, in reality, showed a lack of energy and alertness. Too much hesitation caused the Netherlands to lose contact with the great powers, and several alliances were formed which omitted the Netherlands as it began to get the reputation of being very indecisive. Misplaced economy of the States General was another factor which accounted for Holland's absence at a number of important negotiations.

It has been considered the main weakness of Holland in this period that it did not hold firmly to the English-Dutch Alliance but only supported it in a half-hearted way hovering between reasons of state and reasons of commerce. However, the relations between the Netherlands in matters of trade, colonial policy and finance were so intricately interwoven that the ties between them continued although to a lesser degree than might have been desirable. Fundamentally, nothing had changed in the political aspects of the Netherlands, but the Dutch themselves did not show the same intelligence and perseverance in safeguarding their position as they had in the preceding century. While the Republic had acted to defend its interests in the seventeenth century, it had to be prompted and urged on several occasions to take any action, even in such important matters as the French occupation of Belgium.

On the whole, the policy was one of annoying nobody and keeping away from all entanglements. It was the beginning of the trend toward neutrality and abstinence which would dominate Dutch policy completely in a later period.

It is debatable whether Holland, in that time, would have been capable of a more active policy as the power of the surrounding nations was increasing constantly and, as she was, thus, less able to use her power effectively. It was then, however, unwise to create the impression of being unwilling to take at least the risk of defending one's interest, and the reputation of a republic of merchants, which Holland had gradually acquired, did not increase its respect among the nations. For instance, there is no way of explaining the lukewarm attitude of the Dutch toward the expansion of French might except as a lack of interest in their national power.

While Holland hesitated and worried about its economic position, a new and more energetic nation grew into a major European power: Russia. This meant that on its eastern border as well, the Republic had to count with a strong power instead of with a number of small and ineffective states. The greatest danger of succession of the King of Russia was avoided, but it had become too late to counteract the unification policy of Russia.

The first war in which Holland remained neutral, the Seven Years War, marked the end of Holland as a European power of importance. England prevented Holland's trade because it aided the enemy while the policy of neutrality did not make Holland win the friendship of France. It was the final proof that a weak attitude can never yield any positive results. The French-English War was the culmination of this national short-sightedness.

The final decay of the Alliance among the sea powers undermined the foundation of Holland's independence. The end of the eighteenth century demonstrated clearly that the domination of one power on the European continent spelled Holland's doom. It is the balance of power on the continent and its unity with the sea powers which are the main pillars of its existence.

When France gained the hegemony in Europe, Holland's downfall became a matter of time as she was the natural foothold of the sea powers on the continent. Any nation out to destroy England cannot disregard the key position of the Netherlands as the Germans were to demonstrate a century and a half later.

It was largely the fault of the Dutch merchants that the ties with England had been weakened, and the Francophiles in Holland realized too late that the French revolution was a nationalist one, although its ideology operated with general principles.

In the period of the Batavian Republic, a semblance of Dutch independence was maintained although Holland's power was already almost completely under French supremacy. The danger that Holland would be used as a starting point for an English invasion, and the pro-English sentiment of a sizeable part of the population, finally led to the complete annexation of Holland in 1810.

The supremacy of France had inevitably led to the downfall of Holland, and the return to a balance-of-power system in 1813 automatically led to its resurrection. The end of the freedom of Europe meant the end of Holland's freedom and the regained independence of Europe had, of necessity, to include a free Netherlands. The Dutch had had opportunity to learn once more that the interests of the leading powers demanded a free Holland, but, also, that their own national strength was of the greatest importance. In other words, passivity alone would not guarantee Holland's place among the nations: it required the continued national efforts of the nation itself.

With the lesson in mind that a weak Holland was a danger to the stability of Europe, the great powers as well as the leaders of Holland's independence, were eager to create a country stronger than before. It had also become evident that England was the nation with which Holland's interests were most closely aligned. The absence of a dominant power on the continent was as necessary for Holland as it was for England. Russia, also, had become increasingly aware that the Netherlands were a natural protection for northern Germany.

It was the Prince of Orange, later King William I, who realized that the threat of France had stressed the importance of Holland for the balance of power, and who cleverly used this trend to strengthen the position of his country. Independence with sufficient power to safeguard it was the principle which was going to guide Holland's future. Powers which were neither too weak nor too strong were needed to check the influence of the big nations.

The establishment of a firm, centralized government, a defensible border-line and return of the colonies were deemed necessary to give Holland sufficient strength. The union with Belgium was decided on to create a counterweight against possible French aggression. It is interesting to note now that the plans included the left bank of the Rhine up to Cologne. This, and other plans, came to naught through the opposition of Russia, but the Prince of Orange persisted in his attempts to have Belgium united with the Netherlands as he believed that this would have military as well as economic advantages.

It was England's desire to keep the Netherlands a strong maritime power which would not feel the need to look for support from a continental power. The restoration of the colonies was absolutely essential for this purpose, and its necessity was fully realized by England.

In the nineteenth century the Dutch considered it their main function to be a point of rest in the complicated mechanism of European power politics. Although the Netherlands did not seek a declaration of permanent neutrality nor ever made one themselves, it became more and more their policy to stay out of all European conflicts. Every time that Holland took an active part in European politics, the nation showed sharp disapproval except in the case of the Boer Wars when the situation was reversed.

Through this pronounced tendency toward abstinence from European politics, Holland became a center for the promotion of international law and added to its reputation by the conferences of 1899 and 1907.

Holland's development in the nineteenth and twentieth century was stable and gradual until the supremacy of a new power began to threaten once more the balance of power in Europe. This time it was Germany who, having achieved unity in 1870, was determined to become the leading power and set about this task with energy and military might although with a considerable lack of judgment and without any moral justification. Thus, we see once more the same pattern in Holland's policy: a strong tie with England as the strongest maritime power and friendship with the second-strongest power on the continent: France.

In retrospect the separation of Belgium from the Netherlands may have been a disadvantage to the balance of power in Europe as it reduced Holland definitely to the rank of a small nation. In Holland, as well as in Belgium, voices were raised which pointed to the desirability of maintaining unity, and the great powers admitted the *fait accompli* of the separation only reluctantly. To a certain extent, the declaration of the permanent neutrality of Belgium by the great powers was meant as a return to the barrier system which safeguarded the Netherlands in earlier centuries.

To some extent, Holland drifted once more toward the position it held in the eighteenth century with the difference that now its preference for neutrality and pacifism had at least somewhat more foundation in world trends than in the past although it was a world of the future of which too many Dutchmen were thinking. The lack of interest in really national politics and the indifference toward maintaining a sizeable army and navy were still more a sign of weakness than of idealism, or at least, once again too much preponderance of economic interests over political actualities.

The awareness of the danger of a new conflict in Europe, due to the growing power of Germany, became stronger in the beginning of the twentieth century and even some decades earlier. The pan-Germanic writings and the power-through-strength philosophy were too indicative of things to come to be overlooked. A few times Holland showed its determination to withstand German arrogance although the cultural influence of the Germans was steadily increasing, and in scientific and military circles there was an undeniable admiration for German achievements.

It was not due to any unusual statementship on the part of the Dutch that Holland did not become involved in World War I, but purely to accidental factors of a military nature which made the conquest of Holland irrelevant. A revised von Schlieffen plan envisaged a flank attack on France through Belgium, but not as the original plan through the southern part of Holland. If the Germans had won the war, they would undoubtedly have annexed Belgium which would have made the position of Holland as untenable as that of Czechoslovakia after Munich. For this reason also, as well as to keep a neutral country open as a source of possible supplies, Germany did not invade the Netherlands.

On several occasions in World War I, the neutrality of Holland was severely threatened, and each time for the same reason, viz., that either Germany or England feared that Dutch territory was included in operational plans of the enemy.

The defeat of Germany and the disappearance from the continent of a power striving for European supremacy made Holland breathe easily. But, this time the respite was short, as it took Germany only 25 years to become a menace once more—and a much more dangerous one to the peace of Europe and the world.

This amazing recovery was achieved by the creation of a new philosophy which, by reviving the concept of nationalism in an era which was looking for world organization, and by adopting a new economic and social philosophy together with a complete denial of all concepts of morality, achieved the creation of a more perfect machine for aggression than the world had known before.

The ideological influence of this new brand of pan-Germanism was small in the Netherlands as it was too unbalanced to possess any attractiveness for a coordinated community. It was, in fact, so extravagant that it was not sufficiently believed and did not lead to proper counteraction in Western Europe in the beginning.

It was realized, however, that the strong fortifications along the French and Belgian borders were arguments for a return to the original von Schlieffen plan which envisaged an attack north of the route used in 1914.

The Netherlands maintained a policy of strict neutrality in order to avoid provocation, but it was no surprise when the attack finally came on May 10, 1940. The Netherlands Foreign Minister, Dr. E. van Kleffens, sharply rebuked the German assertion that the attack was justified by secret military arrangements with the Allies.

During the war, the Dutch government announced repeatedly from London that henceforth Dutch foreign policy would be active instead of passive. It was felt that the active participation in the war, the numerous losses of life and goods gave Holland a right to make its voice heard in the shaping of the post-war world. In a recent book on Dutch Foreign Policy, *Buitenlandse Politiek van Nederland* by P. J. Schmidt, now with the United Nations, this point is brought out very strongly although as Holland is not within the realm of power politics, her activities can be mostly in the form of a very active support of international organizations in which her voice, as always, is considered to be of importance, due to her considerable contributions to international law and international agreements.

Schmidt indicated three points as the main purposes of Dutch foreign policy:

1. Maintenance of an independent national existence.

2. Assistance in the bringing about and maintenance of a just and lasting peace.

3. Collaboration in the creation of an efficient interna-

tional legal organization and in an international social, economic organization.

Schmidt remarks correctly that there is not a great theoretical difference between these purposes and pre-war foreign policy, except that the abandoning of the idea of neutrality necessitates a more active participation in international matters. It is a matter of difference in degree rather than of difference in principle.

It is of considerable interest to investigate how the postwar world order affects the traditional principles of Dutch foreign policy. Guided by Van Hamel, we have tried to outline how Holland's existence has been dependent in the past upon the balance of power on the European continent. A dominating power has invariably led to the downfall of Holland while in the long run, friendship with England and the second strongest power on the continent has proved the best safeguard of Holland's independence. Now that the entire power constellation of the world has changed, these former principles have only a very limited validity.

It is undeniable that the world at the moment presents a picture of spheres of influence of the two major powers, the United States and Russia, which cuts clearly across Europe. It is to be hoped that gradually the power factor will lessen in importance and that the power of a clearly defined world law will become stronger. A country like Holland is obviously strongly interested in friendly ties and economic contacts with all nations but many of its more immediate interests are closely connected with the maritime nations, as they were with England in the past. This, however, in a peaceful world would mean economic and cultural rather than political ties.

The power structure inside Europe has relatively lost importance in the world, as supremacy on the European continent hardly means world supremacy any longer so that there is little reason to expect that the relative significance of the various countries will undergo any very fundamental change.

Those countries which are dependent largely on foreign commerce and overseas trade have a larger variable element in their economic structure than those who are more self-sufficient or engaged in trade with adjacent territories, but as long as the former can achieve a fair degree of prosperity there is no reason to assume that economic problems would lead to political complications.

We can arrive only at the same result, viz., that an effective world organization will be the fundamental condition for a continued independent existence of the smaller nations while, without recourse to such a body, power politics would undoubtedly be unable to provide any satisfactory structure. Security in international life is the first condition for national economic prosperity which, in return, guarantees political continuity and stability.

CHAPTER IX

Culture and Economic Wealth

ACCORDING TO HELPFUL Webster, culture is "the complex of distinctive attainments, beliefs, traditions, etc., constituting the background of a racial, religious or social group." As is generally true, when we are desirous of applying such a beautiful and learned definition, we feel a certain vagueness or even a sudden blank.

Thinking of an average Dutchman walking down the streets of Amsterdam, there is a slight hesitation in us before we would like to find out what goes on inside this fellow's mind. Imagine that he is just plain hungry or thirsty or possibly having other animalistic impulses. We would have to bring ourselves to a very high intellectual level to find out in what way his motives are colored by beliefs, traditions, etc. In the old days, we could have said that this Dutchman surely would not be thinking about paprika schnitzel or chili con carne but even that, in our advanced stage of civilization, is no longer a matter of certainty. In fact, he might be humming to himself "Dinah, is there anyone finah in the state of Carolina" and be so breezy as to order a "gin and it." Of course, there are the simpler souls who have not benefited by the blessings of the modern world and who do not go to see French movies, American movies or English movies, or who listen to Bach, Copeland or Schostakovitch or Ravel but they have become so few that even in the backwoods we might hear a radio blare forth:

"It is nice out in the woods today
But it is safer to stay at home."

Although *Teddy Bear's Picnic* is really a delightful little tune.

Should we argue with the philosopher, Scheler, who sharply condemned these aspects of modern civilization and considered it a pure affectation to enjoy St. Francis of Assisi today and Hemingway tomorrow?

Is it really all a lack of cultural integrity, as the good philosopher thought, the antics of a trained monkey going through his daily routine? But we must be careful not to start longing for the primitive stages of civilization or pretty soon we would be accused of neo-vitalism—a polite word for early senility or even worse things.

Culture must be taken with all the bitterness of a medicine because it leads us to - - ? Where exactly does it lead us?

Suppose that it really leads us only to think before we act, that it stifles our impulses in the interests of others which are ultimately ours. Wasn't that the sort of feeling when we yawned our days away on the benches of our beloved educational institutions, hailing the teacher as the one who tamed us and took away our liberty? On the other hand, vacations could grow long and the forests and moors, first full of the unknown and with a promise of adventure, would suddenly look familiar and dull.

Perhaps there is a sort of natural mechanism in us which makes us do things and work for others but at the same time get a sort of happiness out of a life which can be called the operational minimum happiness. We sputter, groan, complain and then we move forward or backward a little.

It would be a horrible thought that we really do more what we like to do than we think because, if true, this leaves us no room for criticism.

However, let us say that culture has the function of putting a certain restraint on the human being, a kind of restraint which we weave patterns of thought around in order to embellish it but which works for the benefit of mankind, however oppressive it may be to the sensitive or artistic individual.

There have been tremendous changes in the amount and intensity of restraint which social groups put on their members. In fact, it has been said that social control has lessened and that we have gained greater freedom.

This would mean that our contacts with our fellow beings have diminished which is a very debatable idea.

What has changed may be the tension of the human mind. The immense fear of things to come which characterized the Middle Ages, the lust for life of the seventeenth and eighteenth centuries are alien to us. We dream of order, stabilization and peace in the world, with little attention for the hereafter and with a reluctance in most of us to reach out for more than a fair share of the goods of this world. Our world is not highly imaginative, not filled with worries about the angels dancing on the tip of a needle and also devoid of a lust for conquest. Mature, well mannered, not particularly adventurous, fairly industrious, fairly well behaved, fairly intelligent, characterizes most of our contemporaries.

An atomic bomb may upset this pattern and give modern life unheard-of dimensions but as long as our genius is purely negatively applied, there seems to be no reason for special applause. So far, it has turned out to be a particularly nasty bomb while all the writings about the splitting of atoms have not made more sense to the average person than they did before.

Our mastery over the physical world does not appear to lack much and human and social problems are of an immeasurably greater importance for our future than producing more goods in less time. In fact, it has become very astonishing to the author that there are still people who believe that the development of more needs creates greater happiness.

Our fundamental needs are very simple and as we have sufficient technical mastery to satisfy them, it seems high time to devote ourselves to the more interesting aspects of life or just to relax and remember that none of us is very interesting or important or different from other people.

When in Western Holland the winter of 1944 dragged on interminably, with the people on the verge of starvation, there was nothing left in their minds but the idea of getting food. They would limp along the barren hostile roads, threatened by German raiding parties, to collect a little food which they could sell as dearly as the traffic would bear or use themselves. When this primary need was again filled, all secondary wishes came to the fore: for housing, clothing, all the small necessities of life, for books, newspapers, music, travel, sports and all those things which make up the life of a modern human being.

These desires have led to great activity and to amazing results, but why should this activity return with the same intensity after all essential needs have been filled? "Getting and spending, we lay waste our power."

Can't we expect, if the world remains free of conflict, a return to a state of happy contentment, of an easily flowing life where work and play and diversion are intermixed in a happy balance? Nobody expects Holland to want to conquer the world nor to give up its place under the sun which it gained after a struggle of many centuries. Nobody should too easily suspect any country of wanting to conquer anything.

Why should we fear the monotony of happiness? Happiness knows neither time nor space nor does it wear. For the first time since the days of antiquity or the days of the primitives, we may learn to regain the feeling for the rhythm of life which we have lacked so sadly for centuries. We may become aware of the utter coarseness of our ways and make life once more into a graceful art, trying to create eternal variety on the same underlying pattern.

The chimes in the tower of our garden suburb will call us in the morning, and, driving along the winding parkways, we will reach the city of tomorrow with its high towering

l be the
art of the suburbs, while the theatre will once more take the
lead as a more accomplished art of infinitely finer touch.

And perhaps we should not shrink from the colorless variety of modern art which may ultimately blend into a world
art when we need Finnish at 8:30, French twenty minutes
later and Russian after the intermission.

The variety placed on a general human pattern can only
help to give color to our lives.

It should be possible to achieve happiness on our slowly
circling globe by giving everybody a chance to find satisfaction in some activity, be it his work or his hobby. There will
be more sports for the sports fans, more different stamps for
the stamp collectors, good and bad books for those who like
to read them, countries to travel to by air, by ship, by rail,
by horse, by foot, by ski, jobs to choose in all seven corners
of the world; in short, a tremendous variety of intellectual
experience which in our advanced stage of civilization, will
mean emotional experience at the same time.

And why should we wish to advance beyond that, once the
current breed of remaining neurotics dies out. Happiness
knows neither time nor space, nor does it wear.

This world of the future will need to reach its perfection
in the leading countries of the world, with the sustained
applause of the others which will bring their achievements
before the forum of the major ones.

Will the cultural achievements of a country be conditioned
by economic factors? This problem is of deep concern to
Europe today. There is an underlying fear in many Europeans that, with the waning of Europe's power, there will
be little room left for cultural activities.

It has been pointed out that we can observe often that the

peak of a nation's political and economic power is accompanied by its greatest attainments in the arts and sciences.
This holds true for Rome and Greece, for the Golden Age
of Holland as well as for England and France in their period
as top nations. On the other hand, it would undoubtedly be
possible to find exceptions as, for instance, the Middle Ages
where great mystics lived in relatively obscure surroundings
or periods. Yet, there is in the first place a *petitio principii*
in this whole matter.

It is obvious that a prosperous country has better possibilities to preserve and distribute their art than a less wealthy
one even if these works are not of overwhelming merit. In
this way an artificial demand is wasted while works which
have possibly more merit may pass unnoticed. On the other
hand, the production of a work of art is not merely a matter
of talent but also a matter of energy and skill. In a period of
great national efforts, there is an atmosphere of activity and
energy which undoubtedly carries the artist along too, although he may violently disagree with the trend of his time.
At the same time, a highly integrated society will place more
skills at the artist's disposal than a less developed one. Thus,
there are two factors—there may be easily others—which
would explain why art and science would reach a higher
level in times of prosperity and power than in those of decline.
Generally speaking, it is true that periods of regression have
shown few remarkable achievements.

Thus, there seems validity in Europe's fear that the decrease
in its political and economic power would mean a decline in
cultural and scientific achievements. But there is another
element in this problem which should not be overlooked.
We see these matters too easily in the light of national power.
In a period of power politics, it is obvious that the energy of
a nation is directed toward the acquisition of power. Great
national energy expresses itself in great national power. If,
as we all hope, the mentality of the world changes in such a

way that national energy will be directed towards the well being of the world in general, or, at least to a certain extent, there would be a new aspect in this entire situation.

A nation, which felt in the past that it lacked weight to make itself heard in the world, might find such spiritual support in the idea of a legal world order—however remote this may seem at the moment—that it will take greater pride in each possible peaceful achievement than it would under conditions which actually meant a severe psychological handicap.

National inferiority and superiority complexes which have great impact on the individual citizen would diminish in a world in which nations know one another better and work toward another goal. This would mean that the pressure in a nation of medium or small strength on the individual citizen would lessen. We see this process in the making at present: there are more international cultural contacts than ever existed before and this means that the individual artist or scientist can find outlets beyond his own nation which did not exist before or at any rate to a lesser extent. Translations of books, production in other countries of music or plays, exhibitions of paintings and sculpture are all on the increase. A more united world will mean a larger market for the artist or scientist.

This factor may offset the decline in power of some regions in the world and even act as a stimulus to regain some of this power by artistic and scientific work. Spiritual and mental power can be of the greatest importance and may give far greater significance to a country than can be expressed by its size or the number of people who inhabit it.

This possibility of a change in the relationship between political and economic power on one side and cultural achievements on the other side may prove to be of great influence on the mentality of Europe. It has very strong cultural traditions which offer a marvelous foundation for new achievements if spiritual factors do not kill these desires too early. In fact, there is a general yearning for a renaissance of the European spirit, as a reaction to the tremendous sufferings which this continent has undergone. At present there is a certain vagueness in this general feeling which has still to crystallize into concrete achievements.

It is natural that the people should feel that so much has been taken away from them that the spirit of Europe is one of the few things which is left to them. It is possible that such an attitude would only lead to imitations of former works of art but also that, if sufficiently strong talents develop, they will find new forms of expression on the basis of a rich cultural heritage. England and France have shown examples of this cultural creativeness, born partly of a desire for reassertion and it is quite possible that the other countries will follow.

The post-war period has brought a tremendous curiosity about literature, theatre, film, music and other forms of art: a curiosity which ended temporarily in a negative way as the quantity of post-war productions could not conceal the fact that their quality was rather disappointing. And yet good art has been produced underground: as far as Holland is concerned mostly in poetry. As an example the poem, *The Song of the Eighteen Dead,* by Jan Campert may be cited. The poet was executed by the Germans. The translation is by Professor C. MacInnes and E. Jansen.

The Song of the Eighteen Dead
A cell two metres long for me,
Two metres, broad as well,
That plot of earth will smaller be
Though where I cannot tell;
But there unknown my rest I'll take
My comrades with me slain,
Eighteen strong men saw morning break—
We'll see no dawn again.

Oh bright and lovely land farewell;
Farewell free dunes and shore.
I vow that from the hour you fell
I thought of ease no more.
What can a loyal man and true,
At such a time essay,
But bid his wife and child adieu
And fight the useless fray?

Hard was my task, my duty stern,
It brought me toil and strife,
But yet my heart would never turn
Back to my easy life.
Freedom was once in Netherland
Both honored and maintained,
Until the savage spoilers' hand,
Its dwelling place profaned.

In fiction it may be still too early to separate the true
from the false, or the artist may have to gain distance from
his emotions, as only a few war novels have come from Europe
so far which are above average.

The relation between art and economic life in Holland
offers some interesting sidelights on the ideas which were
brought to the fore. It is remarkable that painting has been
overwhelmingly developed in the Netherlands in comparison with other forms of art. Hardly anyone would think of
Holland without the idea of one of the familiar scenes which
the Dutch painters immortalized: the colorful vitality of seventeenth century Holland with its background of stately
cities and peaceful canals. Why painting took such a predom-
inant place in Holland is a philosophical problem. Perhaps
it was because the mind turned early to the reality of the
world but in a period when it meant a spiritual struggle to
grasp reality, when only a genius like Rembrandt could cap-

ture in colors a world of which mankind was still afraid. It needed the magnificent clairvoyance of these paintings to take one further step toward this world for which the exact scientists were striving in their field. It is not a coincidence that Rembrandt, Vermeer, Frans Hals and Ruysdael lived in the same period as the famous scientists Huygens, Boerhave, Leeuwenhoek, Stevin and other famous scholars. The flowering of the spirit of a nation is never limited to one field: it leaps to a peak of energy which demonstrates itself in many fields but not everywhere in equal intensity. The turn toward reality as a means and as a purpose was more intense in Holland than anywhere else: the reality which was still existent in the underlying pagan spirit of medieval Europe and which could come to the fore once more when the dualism of the Middle Ages gradually changed into an attempt at unification of the spirit.

The strong light and shadow of the medieval mind began to permit greater differentiation toward the seventeenth century. Its extremes were caught in an intermediary level which allowed room for action. Not the tortured attitude which sees the existing world as a shameful passage toward greater perfection, but a desire, still hesitant, still with many reservations, for the actual physical world, for expansion, for exploration, for greater individual freedom in the metaphysical realm of the mind which actually meant a lesser interest in its problem. Control is strongest where man's strongest interests lie. A cry for freedom in a certain field often means an almost undiscernable step toward control in another field which is first felt as a combined effort instead of a burden.

Protestantism, economic expansion, the exact sciences, humanism are the ideas which guided Holland's steps toward freedom. They were all invariably interconnected, all stages of the same process, a change in the dimensions of the mind which brought the earth closer and the heavens farther. These changes, praised or deplored, considered progressive

or a lack in organic thinking, mean ultimately that the pro-
jection into the future of the human mind diminishes.   •

To think less about our transcendental life may not seem
to have a direct psychological implication but it has. The
domination of our thinking by a future world means a
departure from reality which would make it at the same time
more bearable if not sufficiently mastered. The temporiza-
tion of our goals makes us take the step toward eternity in
reality which we avoid spiritually. Thus, our progress is
at the same time a process of aging anthropologically, a process
which might some time be the subject of an exact investigation and the attempt of cultural forecasting.

The unfolding of the spirit means ultimately a loss, a
transformation into other forms of energy which possibly
might or should diminish the original energy. The greater
tension, the greater fear of the Middle Ages, the tremendous
but playful energy of the classics are gone to return no more.

In this chain of development, the turn of the mind toward
the physical world was problematical, laden at times with
pitfalls into spiritual doubt, in the new era. Therefore, perhaps, its cultural life became intensely colorful, multiform,
full of innovations and of amazing vanity. The lack of one-
ness of purpose: the existence of the Puritan next to the
worldly merchant, of the humanist, full of the zest for an
erudite life, next to the mystic, of the exact scientist next to
the thundering priest deepened the dimensions which a
period of less conflicts would not have known.

If we see the New Era as a period of the adolescence of
Western civilization, it carries all the elements of the future
in it while only its negation can be an indication of the aspects
which may be lost in later stages. In our present day, it remains too difficult to visualize the tremendous advantage
which the European mind held over that of other continents
and which was caused, in the first place, by its superiority in
the exact sciences and its greater knowledge of reality. Of

this knowledge, which gave them the mastery of the earth, it is interesting to put the question whether the loss of power was caused by the loss of knowledge or vice versa. Knowledge of reality should include in this case knowledge of human relations. As the turn of the spirit toward the world undoubtedly involves a greater interest in our fellow beings, and our desire for technical mastery leads to the necessity of fitting human beings into the processes which are necessary for this goal.

Perhaps seventeenth century Holland again furnishes a good example of this. In its period of expansion and explorations, it had a more intense community life than it has known ever since. Today, in the United States, relations of people with one another are far more numerous than in Europe, and newly arrived Europeans are apt to comment upon what they consider lack of reserve or privacy.

When Europe began to freeze into a caste system, it was sowing the seeds of its own decay. Once the human mind becomes set to a pattern in one respect, the same will ultimately result in regard to other matters. There is never complete stabilization of the mind as any emergency will create responses which can neither be controlled nor forseen, at least not at the present stage of knowledge.

However, the loss of mental elasticity is a very considerable factor as it implies a diminishing interest. Interest, or rather awareness that things might be different than they appear to be is at the source of all discoveries and of all innovations. The tendency to regard the world as stable leads to a noticeable decrease in activity.

When there was an almost universal interest in seventeenth century Holland, its entire society was in a state of fluctuation. When the Netherlands became stabilized—forced to adjust itself when the limit of its political expansion was reached—there was an immediate decrease in all fields of activity, including those of the spirit and the mind.

If we transfer these observations to an individual, it is quite understandable that this should be so. An individual has a certain amount of energy at his disposal, all of which he may use to reach his goals in life. If he encounters obstacles which he cannot overcome, the "let down" will not only affect his behavior in regard to the activity in which the obstacle was encountered but his attitude in all fields. The fear that he may lose more than gain if he continues his efforts, leads to a desire to consolidate one's position on a lower level than the one originally aimed for. This being on a lower level carries with it the realization that the use of all available energy is no longer necessary and leads to a lesser effort than the original one.

We see here again that success in one field of endeavor easily leads to success in other fields. It increases confidence although it certainly cannot create talents which are not available but it stimulates them and generates better opportunities for their development.

It is for instance, hard to imagine that the Dutch in the eighteenth century were so different from those of the seventeenth century in regard to talents and ability. The considerable decrease in achievement was largely psychological, due to the realization that the peak of national power had passed and that efforts to regain it could not possibly be successful. This decrease in mental tension leads to a neglect of existing possibilities until a more balanced world in the second half of the nineteenth century offered again better opportunities for peaceful development of the smaller countries. Then the energy of the Dutch which must have been in a latent state soared to a new high. Thus, there is a considerable interaction between the general world constellation and the cultural level of a nation. A more balanced world may bring many untapped possibilities to the fore which will ultimately lead to a new world culture.

The idea that the world has now only two ideologies left

is nonsensical. There are only two at the moment which attract most of the attention but it would be just as possible to say that there are fifty or sixty and it would be a great deal better if people would stare themselves less blind on the two major ones. What about the different world religions and their attitude to social and economic problems, what about the attitude of the smaller countries or those one never learns about?

There is no ideology in the world which favors suppression but certain conditions may make freedom a more distant possibility for some than for others. As soon as economic stability is reached, the idea of power would lose many of its sharp edges.

War has always been fundamentally an economic problem. We exercise power over others for economic ends and by economic means. Economic stabilization—not complete which is impossible but up to a certain level—would make war an act of insanity which would arouse the world sufficiently to take counteraction, and which does not need the guardian power of a few big nations but should be the expression of the will of a united world.

Ideologies are forms of group thinking which do not attract attention until the groups clash for reasons which have nothing to do with their ideologies. When the Roman Catholics and Protestants fought each other bitterly, it was not on account of their ideologies but because the former stood for centralization, the latter for decentralization, and this involved a lot of direct and very concrete problems. The author fails to see completely what advantage there would be in having only one or two ideologies in the world unless they are so vague and general that they become meaningless.

The way of thinking of a group or an individual is the outcome of the structure of his mind and the experiences of his life, and as little subject to a value judgment by others as the sun or the moon.

The trend of looking for conflicting ideologies is purely a trend to look for conflicts. No more, no less. Why this should be necessary in a world which can easily support two billion people in peace, happiness and prosperity seems utterly in-comprehensible.

The only reason is that our thinking is still excessively materialistic, and that we do not ask the question whether we have enough to enjoy our lives but whether somebody else has more. As long as this compulsion neurosis subsists there is little more for mankind to do than take lots of exercise and read very little.

Nobody ever writes in any newspapers about the ideology of the Eskimo, yet he has probably a very interesting one with lots of elements of surprise for us. But nobody seems to worry terribly much whether he enjoys all the catalogued freedoms or possibly a few uncatalogued ones, as, for instance, the right to sleep in his neighbor's igloo when the weather is sub-zero.

If mankind is still in such a primitive stage that it is always necessary to find out who is the strongest for purely academic reasons or the discomfort of smaller nations, it might be possible to invent ingenious devices to test this, or more simply, to say that greatness of spirit would not ask such questions. Or even reason would be sufficient.

Animals of the same kind only fight one another in the mating period. Freud and some other people still like to believe that is the root of many of our troubles. It would be sad, however, if three thousand years of civilization had not taught us to regulate our various impulses. Besides, they have, so it is hardly a problem.

Rests with us only the sad conclusion that mankind is still in a stage of immaturity, and that we can do little except wait for it to grow up a little more.

CHAPTER X

Problem No. 1

THE WAR AND ITS aftermath has made the Dutch much more conscious of their role in the Netherlands Indies. The long period of suppression made people ask themselves many questions in regard to their own national past and their position in the world. There was a very substantial upsurge of national feeling, a greater unity which led to a strong interest in the Indies during the occupation and, obviously, to a certain amount of pride. The Dutch felt that they had no reason to be ashamed of their achievements or methods in the East.

Living in an era of conquest, they obviously forgot some of their former doubts about the rights of Europe to bring the blessings of its civilization to other continents which had not particularly asked for them. Perhaps they had a right to be proud.

In the sixteenth and seventeenth centuries the Dutch did not sail forth as conquerors to other parts of the world. They set out as explorers and merchants, eager for the riches of the tropics and driven by that spirit of a New Era which widened the small world of Western Europe into that of an entire globe. This was hardly a matter of right or wrong as it is difficult to imagine that civilization would have developed otherwise. The pattern of the Middle Ages had lost its appeal, the pattern of the New Era involved expansion and exploration. It also involved suffering and injustice if we want to judge on the basis of our current moral attitude.

It would be erroneous to believe that the people of that period were not aware of the moral implications of their expansion. They had a tendency to believe that it was sufficient to apply Christian morality with moderation, to fellow Christians but not to heathens or pagans. Numerous are the admonitions of those, however, who held higher ideals and saw it as the first purpose of discoverers to bring Christianity to pagan peoples. Which element—the commercial or the spiritual—weighed heavier is an entirely academic question as this depended solely upon the people involved. The happy combination of spiritual ideals and good business sense is a quality which the Dutch have in common with several other nations.

In the heyday of the East India Company, there were never more than about 10,000-15,000 Dutch in the Indies of whom several thousand were probably foreign mercenaries. They certainly did not rule by force and applied it only reluctantly when the necessity arose. The main interest was commerce, and this was often carried out by playing the local princes against one another. European wars were often carried to Asia and gave the natives the edifying spectacle of the various European factions fighting one another while the indigenous population stood by or tried to use these wars to their own advantage.

The high officials of the Netherlands East India Company were reluctant to assume government functions, but they became virtual maharahjas. They exerted feudal power in order to ensure their trade monopolies.

The constant wars and military expenditures used up most of the Company's profits and toward the end of the eighteenth century the Company went bankrupt when the war with England led to a blockade of the Java trade.

The failure of the East India Company resulted in a complete change in the organization of the Indies: the territory was put under direct government control and private enterprise was encouraged to start ventures in the Netherlands Indies.

Before this plan was put into effect, the British seized the Netherlands colonies to protect them from an attack by the French, and Raffles was instituted as the Lieutenant Governor of the Indies.

Raffles followed a fair policy toward the native rulers and succeeded in setting up an efficient colonial administration of which many innovations were retained later.

The Convention of 1814 between Great Britain and the Netherlands restored the Indies to Holland. The Dutch, having emerged as a stronger nation from the Napoleonic Wars, devoted their full energy to an expansion of their administration in the Indies and to gaining control over the Outer Islands. Some of the expansion was achieved by peaceful means; in other cases, long military campaigns proved necessary.

In order to bolster their income from the Indies, the Dutch introduced in 1830 the so-called culture system whereby the natives were obliged to grow certain crops for the government. Although this system has been much criticized —and certainly led to abuses—it also served to bring new crops to the Indies which ultimately added to the prosperity of the Indies.

When the liberal movement gained in strength in the Netherlands, there developed a strong reaction against this system which finally led to its abolishment in 1890. On the whole, the Dutch tried to administer the islands via a system of indirect rule and to let native life develop according to its own patterns.

The progress of political thinking in the Netherlands caused a gradual change in the relations with the Indies. After 1860, the conviction began to grow that the Netherlands had another function beyond increasing the material prosperity of the Indies, mainly with a view to the benefit of the home country. In 1901 the Netherlands government announced that it had a moral duty to fulfill toward the

Indonesian people. This declaration is considered the beginning of the so-called "ethical policy." The interests of the Indonesian people were going to be the main principle of Dutch policy, but it cannot be denied that there was a strong element of paternalism in this attitude. It was still too much the idea that many things should be done for the Indonesians, but not by the Indonesians. However, the greater interest in the people led consequently to the idea that they should have a more active role in their own administration, and in 1916 a "People's Council" was created which was to advise the Governor General in matters of legislation. Although the Council was first composed of a majority of Europeans, it gradually changed until the Indonesians were the largest group, a group, however, which was only partly and indirectly elected by the population. It assumed gradually the function of a legislative body as it became a common law practice for the Governor-General to abstain from overruling its decisions.

The same more liberal trend caused the substitution of the term "overseas territories" for the former expression "colonies" in the constitutional revision of 1922. In addition, the Indonesian Constitution of 1925 transferred the discussion of the annual budget from the Netherlands States General to the People's Council.

It was all indicative of the same trend, a trend whose final aim was no doubt praiseworthy and which led to great achievements in the fields where general and economic interests met, such as hygiene, communications, modernization, etc., but which remained slow where there was no active stimulus as, for instance, in the political and educational fields. This, again, is not a matter where evaluation is fair as such a course of events is entirely normal. Increasing democratization was a process which the Dutch were, in principle, eager to favor but it cannot be overlooked that many group interests ran contrary to this process and were not overly eager to expedite it to any marked degree.

Business interests feared labor conflicts with increasing political influence of the native population while government circles were often very much aware of the potential development of the Indies but visualized much of it as achievable by their own initiative.

However, the stimulus for greater political development came from the population itself.

The history of Indonesian nationalism is one of the gradual and shifting application of Western ideas to a static Eastern civilization, caused by a few leaders who forever were grouping and regrouping their tenets. It started as an Islamic movement, the "Sarekat Islam," but fell rapidly under the sway of Western revolutionary ideas, especially those coming from and encouraged by Russia. The masses of the Indonesian population understood little of the dialectics of Marxism and the early movement remained confined to small groups of intellectuals and native leaders who found some following by projecting the past, the happy Empire of Majapahit, into the future, thus gaining some hold over the Indonesian mind. Support came also from groups who favored the development of trade-unionism and considered it the only road toward greater participation of the Indonesians in economic prosperity, and a way to break the hold of European management on the economic system.

Considerable nationalist agitation developed around 1926 and 1927 when Western capitalism went through one of its most dispirited periods.

The idea of armed revolt led to a reaction, however, as the more moderate native leaders had a chance to come to the fore with a policy which was more realistic under the given conditions.

Dr. Sutomo, the founder of the "Indonesian Study Clubs" and Suwardi Suryaningrat (Dewantoro), the originator of the "Taman Siswa" schools, were the main representatives of this more moderate trend which saw national independence as a more remote ideal.

Between 1922 and 1932, Gandhi's attitude of non-cooperation was followed to a certain extent in the Netherlands Indies, especially as it applied to participation in representative bodies. However, the effort to give Indonesian nationalism a similar form to that of India was not successful, and an "interinsular congress," meant to create a movement similar to the Indian party, did not lead to tangible results.

In 1927 a new political organization, the Partai Nasional Indonesia, came into being under the leadership of Soekarno. Like Sjahrir, the leaders were mostly young university men who had studied in Holland and had been in close contact there with international communist organizations.

The program as outlined by Soekarno stated that: Indonesia should be made independent at once; the Netherlands government would never willingly grant independence nor willingly allow a greater degree of self-government; therefore, the Partai Nasional Indonesia had to be a revolutionary, not an evolutionary organization.

In their methods of propaganda, there was clearly considerable influence of communism. Cells were planted in other parties which were accused of lack of patriotism if they resisted the attempts at unification.

In 1928 a loose federation was formed of most of the political parties by the leadership which, after a secret vote, was entrusted to Dr. Sutomo and not to Soekarno. When the Partai Nasional Indonesia became a more or less destructive influence which was resented by large parts of the native population, the government stepped in and arrested several of its leaders.

The party lost in importance and split two years later into two factions, the Partai Indonesia (Partindo) and the

Pendidikan Nasional Indonesia (National Indonesian Training of the People).

The organization Muhammadiyah developed well in the meantime. It became a large and efficiently organized association which possessed many excellent schools, hospitals, poorhouses, orphanages, Islamic colleges, etc. It came into a serious conflict on Mohammedan matters with the Partai Sarekal Islam, a conflict which made the latter lose considerably in significance.

In 1934 the moderate Indonesian leader Sutomo succeeded in uniting two parties into the Partai Indonesia Raja (Parindra) meaning the Party of Great Indonesia or Great Indonesian Party. It soon became the largest nationalist party although political life, at that time, received serious setbacks from the economic depression which hit the Indies unusually hard.

As the prices of tropical products reached an all-time low, the population lost heavily in earnings and, as much of the economy is based on small debts, the situation became quite difficult.

The government, with the aid of a gift of 25 million guilders from the Netherlands, made great efforts to ease the strain, and the greater collaboration between nationalists and government officials took some of the sharp edges off the nationalist movement.

Another factor which aided in steering nationalism into a more moderate direction was the growing awareness that Indonesian independence would merely tend to make the country subject to Japanese aggression.

The original admiration which the Indonesians had felt for Japan had been superseded by fear of her imperialism. As local autonomy was increased measurably in the late thirties, the feeling grew that an evolutionary attitude was preferable to a radical one.

This moderate trend, certainly to a large extent caused by

the threatening international situation, led, in 1939, to a loose federation of the major political parties: the Gabungan Politiek Indonesia (Gapi Indonesian Political Federation). It included the Partai Sarekat Islam Indonesia, Parindra, Gerindo and Pasendan groups. Although the international situation was too turbulent to cause great interest in internal reforms, a program was developed which advocated gradual transition toward a fully responsible native government which would collaborate with Holland in matters of constitutional law, foreign policy and defense.

Although the Gapi did not develop to a noticeable extent, an even larger federation was attempted which included the Gapi, the Gaspi (Federation of Labor Unions) and the Miai (an organization of a number of Islamic societies).

This federation came out in favor of active participation in case of war against Japan, but dissension again arose, and not much was made of the potential willingness of the Indonesian people to take part in the defense of their homeland.

On the whole, it can be said that the nationalist movement in 1940 and until the invasion was definitely anti-Japanese and believed that a course of collaboration with the Dutch would ultimately prove the best way toward a status of greater or complete independence, with a certain integration into the Netherlands Kingdom.

After the Netherlands had been invaded, it became a matter of crucial importance to ascertain in what measure the collaboration between the various population groups could be fostered. The government was not prepared to initiate substantial reforms while the country was at war, but it did realize the urgent need to prepare for later reforms.

To this end a commission of seven members, three Dutch, three Indonesian and one Chinese Indonesian, was instituted under the chairmanship of Dr. F. Visman to study what political trends were present among the population. It has been considered a drawback of their report that it does not make clear what group a certain spokesman represents and what weight this group actually carries.

The first volume depicts the development of the Indies between the two World Wars while the second one discusses the wishes of various population groups against this background. It furnishes an interesting overall analysis of the attempts at harmonization of Western and Eastern civilization. There is no doubt that Indonesian civilization was still dualistic in character as Western economy was superimposed upon the native economy and not sufficiently integrated to give the East Indies economy sufficient stability although the government was making efforts in that direction. It is interesting to note that the national income of the Indies with a population of seventy million was estimated at 2 billion guilders of which 1.4 billion was attributed to the native population. In comparison the income of the Netherlands with 9 million inhabitants was 5 billion guilders.

Yet, the impact of the West was the element which added the dynamic quality to the static society of the East and which created the ideas, even if applied against its own immediate interests, which meant progress and development. This was also evident in the field of education. The Dutch originally meant to leave Indonesian culture undisturbed but the needs of modern economy led to a gradual increase in education which began to move much more rapidly in the last decade.

These processes are brought about by gradual historical changes, and whether Western education in itself is really the height of human achievement is a problem which could be dealt with negatively or positively—in long and learned volumes. But the modernization—which means Westernization—of the world is a process which does not require our approval or disapproval. It is an unavoidable fact.

Nobody could claim that the Dutch East Indies prior to the war were a poorly governed territory. On the other hand, it is equally obvious that a war which upsets the existing order of things acts as a catalyst for social processes which otherwise might require generations.

In a country which is as heterogeneous as the Indies, Dutch rule brought stability and helped to introduce ideas which were originally alien to the East but were essential for its development. It does not have to be argued that a population of seventy millions was not ruled by 250,000 whites by force.

In many cases the local Dutch official took the sharp edges off the native social system and was regarded with great trust by the inhabitants in whom may have lived a vague and remote dream of greater freedom.

The politically conscious group was relatively small. In 1941, the membership of all Indonesian political organiations was estimated at only 115,000. Religious and social-religious associations had about 300,000. Labor organizations had only about 87,500 members. Subscriptions to Malay and Chinese-Malay newspapers came to 53,000, although the number of readers was considerably larger.

Thus, the group which was actively interested in political matters can be estimated at 500,000-1,000,000 which is still a high guess. This group combined with the 250,000 whites and half-castes—they belonged legally to the white population—formed the dynamic element in a population of 70 millions.

This entire category was united in one respect: they all believed in the progress of Indonesia and the possibility of its becoming a progressive and prosperous community.

They had, however, strongly divergent opinions about the way in which this goal could be reached. Western business interests were inclined to believe that business had stimulated the efficient production of numerous products, and, that under a free enterprise system, the country was best served. They tended to overlook that a raw-material economy is particularly vulnerable in times of crisis, but the depression of the thirties brought combined efforts of the government and business to save production of tropical products through a certain amount of stabilization. Price-fixing has been charged in several cases but, on the other hand, the drop in prices in the thirties was so great that price regulation then involved prevented the collapse of production.

The idea that the economy should be stabilized by a moderate amount of industrialization in order to produce certain consumer goods locally was more favored by government economists than by business, which was obviously not greatly in favor of the leveling-off of the various economic regions of the world.

The thinking of the Indonesian Nationalists ran more along political than economic lines but it was undoubtedly easier for them to find a common meeting ground with the government economists than with leaders of private business. The idea of making Indonesia less of a pure raw-material economy was favorably regarded by the Indonesian population and is probably the principle which will be followed now by a more autonomous Indonesia.

The influence of socialist thinking in the nationalist movement has probably increased, compared with thinking along Mohammedan and racial lines.

The Indonesian leaders are quite aware that greater autonomy of the Indies will mean increased—not decreased—Westernization of the East. It is an odd paradox that this process will need the aid of the West but it also shows that the future means more ties between both parts of the world, although of a different nature. Increased prosperity and a certain amount of equalization may mean less political contact but it definitely will bring an increase in economic and cultural relations. A more developed economy will lead to greater integration into a regional as well as into the world economy.

Thus, finally the war will not cause a reversal of previously existing trends but mainly their intensification and their realization at an increased tempo. Periods of stagnation and regression will undoubtedly come as the struggle between static and dynamic elements will bring a structural reorganization of society which cannot be expected to come about without friction and difficulty.

If we visualize the picture at the moment the war broke out, we come more or less to the following results:

The great masses of the population lived a simple rural life without hardships but also without luxuries. Their contact with the West was the possibility to work on plantations or factories or to raise certain products for export.

Although the wages for their types of work were low—according to Western standards—it raised those who took part in it above the great masses of the population and gave them a chance to achieve greater material welfare than their neighbors. The work for Western enterprise was often seasonal, and this must be born in mind when considering statistical data. In 1930 the number of workers was estimated at 20,871,000, distributed as follows:

Agriculture	14,363,000
Industry	2,208,110
Transportation	316,100
Commerce	1,293,300
Liberal professions	169,500
Public administration	516,200
Other occupations	2,003,200

As only 3.83 per cent of the inhabitants of the Indies lived in places of more than 50,000 inhabitants, it is obvious that these activities were largely conducted in rural areas. The largest city, Batavia, had over half a million inhabitants but there were only six other cities in the entire archipelago which had over one hundred thousand inhabitants.

Thus, native life took place mainly in the native village, the dessa, dominated by religion and custom, and flowed along easily and harmoniously in one of the world's most beautiful and most fertile countries. There was an element of eternity about the life of the natives which may have made the impact of the West a factor which barely touched the surface.

The Westerners who liked and understood the Indonesians were liked and respected in return; those who regarded it merely as a field for profitable economic activity were probably regarded with indifference, or if they were ill-mannered or coarse, they were probably despised and hated. The West sent over many of its representatives: government officials, business people, doctors and engineers, missionaries, fortune-seekers and many others. The high intellectual level and the excellent training of Dutch officials has done much to create real understanding between Indonesians and Dutch, while the technical and professional achievements of the West not only aided the natives but also commanded the respect of the more progressive elements.

Excellent communications, beautiful roads, public hygiene, experimental stations for agriculture and industry have been elements of progress by which all groups of the population profited.

On the cultural level the impact was rather small. In many cases the Dutch profited from their contact with the East, and Holland has produced, ever since the seventeenth century an amazing number of outstanding scholars on Oriental affairs. The work of the Dutch in native law has been praised all over the world.

Of the Indonesian uppercrust small numbers studied at Dutch universities and became so completely Westernized that they do not strike a Dutchman as being foreign. The writings of Sjharir, for instance, breathe a completely Western progressive spirit in which it is hard to detect an alien or Oriental element. However, these cultural contacts were restricted to very small groups, and it is perhaps even possible to say that the cultural impact of the Indies on Holland was greater than vice versa. Multatuli, one of Holland's greatest writers, is not thinkable without the East. This holds also true for Cuperus, Augusta de Wit, H. Borel and the modern writers Du Perron and Fabricius. Indonesian literature continued largely in traditional lines and shows only a few Westernized figures like Princess Kartini and Noto Soeroto. Western and Eastern music had practically no contact points, and the Javanese Wajang-plays were a curiosity to the Westerner except to those few who possessed a thorough knowledge of Javanese history and literature.

The desire of the government to acquaint the Indonesians with Western thinking led to the establishment of the Bureau of Popular Literature which produced translations of masterworks of Western literature. It can be assumed that these writings become a living reality to only a few people although, on the whole, they were ready to see what foreigners were like. It is also hard to imagine what the impact of Western movies on the Eastern mind has been. It seems impossible that there would be a real understanding—provided movies ever require any real understanding—but they certainly did not serve to impress the East with the manners, virtues or good taste of the West.

The experience of the Bureau of Popular Literature was that the greatest success was achieved with the old native stories in prose and poetry which have appeared in hundreds of different versions in the course of time. Shadow-plays, myths, local legends, fairy tales and legendary adventures flourished far better in the Archipelago than Dickens or Jack London, whether it was highly refined Javanese poetry, doggerels or rhymed folk-tales.

There was a large residue in the Eastern mind which the West never penetrated and perhaps should not try to penetrate as it could be argued that it was on a higher level or, at any rate, much closer to the heart of the Indonesian.

Thus, we get the picture of a society which moves fundamentally along well-established lines of custom and religion, blessed by natural conditions which forever exempt it from spending 90 per cent of its energy on economic matters and 10 per cent on the pursuit of happiness.

The division of percentages for the Indies is a happier one and even if the demands of the twentieth century may change this somewhat, we should wish that the Indies may preserve as much as possible of its own life, progressing further along the trends which were present before the war with the aid of all groups who had the real interests of the Indies at heart.

CHAPTER XI

When War Came to the Indies

ON DECEMBER 7, 1941, came the treacherous attack of Japan on Pearl Harbor. Immediately afterwards the Netherlands government in London declared war on the Japanese Empire.

In his announcement of this decision, Governor General A. W. C. Tjarda van Starkenborgh Stachower said:

"People of the Netherlands East Indies: In its unexpected attack on American and British territories, while diplomatic negotiations were still in progress, the Japanese Empire has consciously adopted a course of aggression. These attacks which have thrown the United States of America and the British Empire into active war on the side of already fighting China, have as their object the establishment of Japanese supremacy in the whole of east and southeast Asia. The aggressions also menace the Netherlands East Indies in no small measure. The Netherlands Government accepts the challenge and takes up arms against the Japanese Empire."

Full mobilization of the army was ordered immediately and defense forces were sent into the Outer Possessions to guard against attacks.

The Netherlands East Indies army was estimated at a strength of about 100,000-125,000 men, including home guards and militia. The nucleus of the army consisted of professional soldiers, many of them Amboynese and Menadonese. All able-bodied Netherlanders in the Netherlands East Indies had been conscripted about a year earlier. By a law of July 11, 1941, conscription had been extended to the native part of the population as well, but through lack of equipment and some hesitancy on the part of the government, only small contingents of this native militia were inducted into the army towards the end of October, 1941.

Good progress had been made with the mechanization of the army while the air force consisted of about 250-300 planes, many of them, however, almost obsolete. Much equipment that had been ordered did not arrive on time in the Indies.

The greatest part of Duch naval strength, consisting of five cruisers, seven destroyers, over twenty submarines and a number of smaller craft was concentrated in the Indies.

When the war with Japan broke out, all Japanese citizens were interned immediately. The interned group consisted of 1069 Japanese, 301 Formosans and 25 suspect Europeans.

The Netherlands East Indies Army planes went to the aid of the British in Malaya while Naval units were despatched to Singapore: on December 13 naval forces sank four Japanese army transports off the coast of Thailand, while, from then on, news about the sinking of Japanese ships became almost a daily item.

The Indonesian political parties issued a statement in which they urged the people "to render all possible assistance to the government in maintaining order and to keep calm."

Occasional Japanese air attacks were the only enemy activity which reached the Netherlands Indies in the first period.

On January 10, 1942, the all-out war on the Indies was started when the Japanese launched a full-fledged attack on the Island of Tarakan, off east Borneo, and on three different parts of the Minahassa, the "northern arm" of Celebes. Dutch army and air forces put up strong resistance and damaged several Japanese naval units. The Dutch were quite aware that the odds were strongly against them, but destruction of oil installations and other equipment was carried out according to plan.

Bombing attacks on several points of the Archipelago increased in intensity with the naval base of Ambon as one of the main targets.

Parachutists succeeded in completing the conquest of the Minahassa where infiltration had also been used with some success. Dutch and Australian air forces gave a good account of themselves, and Japanese losses were reported at that time to have been heavy.

A great success was achieved by air attacks on January 23 on enemy naval and transport concentration in Makassar Straits, between Celebes and Borneo. Twelve direct hits were scored on eight Japanese warships and transports. Next day, several transports of the same large convoy were sunk. Attacks on ship concentrations near Balikpapan in Borneo were also successful.

American air and naval forces joined in the various attacks and achieved considerable results with torpedo attacks and bombings.

On January 25, landings on Borneo and at Kandari, in Southern Celebes, took place.

Naval and air resistance to the Japanese invasion continued to inflict serious damage but land resistance was whittled down quickly in most cases by the superiority of the Japanese in numbers and equipment.

Resistance of Netherlands East Indies troops around Balik-papan continued for some time while the scorched earth policy was carried out completely in most regions. Ambon also became the subject of a concentrated attack, while fighting in Celebes continued throughout January.

In the beginning of February air attacks on Java increased in intensity. By that time Borneo was largely in Japanese hands although resistance in the interior continued. Naval activities around Ambon resulted in the sinking of several Japanese cruisers, as well as of a destroyer and a submarine.

On February 14, heavy raids on Palembang, Sumatra, took place which were followed by the landing of paratroops as the Japanese were eager to stop the demolitions of the oil-fields. They succeeded in preventing some of the demolitions, but most of them had been carried out successfully. Around the middle of February fighting around Palembang as well as on Celebes continued.

On February 19, when the Japanese had surrounded Java on all sides, the first reports came in of the arrival of detachments of British, American and Australian troops, however, only in very small numbers. The occupation of Bali caused the Japanese several naval losses.

Air raids continued to be successful and the "ship a day" tradition of the Dutch was kept up pretty well. Official figures on the number of Japanese ships sunk are still not available.

On February 27, strong Japanese formations were reported to be approaching Java. They were attacked repeatedly by Allied squadrons. On the 28th, the first phase in the battle of Java opened when Japanese invasion troops established three beach heads on the north coast.

In this period the Dutch navy, with the naval forces of some of its Allies, played an heroic role. When the news of the attack on Bali came, Admiral Karel Doorman raced his small fleet to the South Cape on Bali, and, in the dark of night, they made a daring attack on the Japanese fleet, the cruiser "De Ruyter" leading, followed by the "Java" and the "Piet Hein," with Dutch and American destroyers making up the rear. When, by firing star shells, the "De Ruyter" could see the enemy, she was too close to train her guns properly. But the "Java" had that chance while the "Piet Hein," coming up astern, caught the withering fire of the 8-inch guns.

Later in the night, a similar attack was made by four American destroyers and the "Tromp." The Japanese took heavy punishment that night in Bandia Strait, but the small fleet of Admiral Doorman was further depleted. He was left with the "De Ruyter," the "Java," the damaged "Houston," the "Perth" and the "Exeter."

On February 26, this fleet was looking for the enemy around Madoera Island. Finally at 4 o'clock, when they were racing northward, the "De Ruyter" sighted the enemy. She opened fire immediately, and in the beginning Allied gunnery was good although the Japanese guns outranged them. One Japanese destroyer was hit, but the "Exeter" was put out of action. The destroyer "Kortenaer," trying to cover her limping retreat, was hit by a torpedo and broke in two. A little later the British destroyer "Electra" fell victim to a Japanese torpedo also. However, in this stage of the encounter, three Japanese destroyers were sunk.

Admiral Doorman in an effort to break off the struggle in which he was so hopelessly outnumbered, tried to find the convoy where he could do more damage. He failed, and later at night he came once more upon the enemy fleet. With all guns blazing, his small force, now entirely without destroyer protection, went into action. Then he flung his force sharply around, but it was too late: torpedoes caught the "Java" as well as the "De Ruyter" and both went down into the blazing sea.

The Allied navy had done all it could to prevent the Japanese landings, and nothing was left to do except the blowing up of all shore installations.

The invasion of the Japanese army was resisted valiantly by the Netherlands East Indies army, reinforced with American, Australian, and British units but the battle was hopeless from the beginning and demoralization set in at an early stage. The air force continued its attacks as long as possible but its strength was wearing down rapidly.

The Japanese fanned out from their three beachheads and succeeded in making pretty steady progress.

On March 3, the Allied Commander, General Archibald P. Wavell, left Java for British India, leaving the command of the Allied forces in the hands of the Dutch.

On the same day, it was admitted that air control had passed into the hands of the enemy.

From that time on, fighting spread throughout the island without taking on a definite front line. The situation had become hectic, and coordination between the defenders was more or less lost.

On March 6, Batavia was evacuated and the government moved to Bandoeng where the last ditch defense was being organized.

The complete control of the air made Allied troop movements practically impossible. On March 7, the northern defenses of Bandoeng were cracked, and the situation was admittedly critical. On March 8, the official radio station at Bandoeng sent its last message: "We are now shutting down. Goodbye until better times. Long live the Queen."

Except for guerilla activity in the outlying possessions, and for some parts of New Guinea, which were not occupied by the Japanese, the entire archipelago was in the hands of the enemy.

The Japanese were surprised about these things in the Netherlands Indies: the European population had stayed behind except for a few high officials whom Governor General van Starkenborgh Stachouwer had sent away in the interests of the country; there was order in the archipelago; the population on the whole was loyal to the Dutch.

As the Japanese regarded the Westerners as the leaders of the East, they began by interning all Europeans and by removing all Dutch signs. The interned Europeans were given small rations but received considerable aid from the Indonesians and the Chinese.

The Japanese started by prohibiting all political activity but on March 9, 1943, they founded the "Poetera," intended as the all-embracing political party. This organization lasted only one year and was replaced by the Djawa Hoko Kai, organizing the Indies as a section of Greater East Asia. The organization was on a cooperative basis, and only those who were members received the materials needed for their occupations. Soekarno was a leading figure in the "Djawa Hoko Kai."

A section of this organization was in charge of anti-air raid activities and became the nucleus of the so-called "Barisan Pelopor," shock troops which in turn became a section of the Republican Army.

The Japanese also trained a police corps, the "Kempetai," (Kempei) who were still in existence in 1945.

All religions were prohibited by the Japanese except the Islam. In 1944 they brought all Mohammedan associations together in one organization, the "Masjoemi" (Masjarakat Oemat Islam) which had a military section, the "Hiezboellah."

In addition to all these semi-military organizations, the Japanese attempted to draft former Netherlands Indies military personnel, but few were willing to sign the declaration of loyalty (soerat soempah). Those who refused were put in concentration camps.

An intensive propaganda campaign was carried out in the native villages and, in some cases, to create contempt for the West, the most abominable methods were used to humiliate European women.

Many Indonesions were drafted into labor organizations, modeled after the Todt organization. These so-called "Heihos" were not volunteers like the "Soekarelas," a sort of S.A. organization which was used for the confiscation of food and other materials, much to the detriment of the native population.

In 1945 this system began to weigh heavily on the population as food shortages began to develop everywhere. The organization charged with the collection of rice became a powerful political organization which had a strong hold on the people. The Japanese were very systematic in their attempts to instill hatred against westerners although their Greater East Asia propaganda had to overcome the centuries-old "adat" of the native population.

The conscription of labor caused great bitterness among the population: of the 68,000 laborers who were used on the Burma and Siam railroads, 17,000 died from starvation. In January, 1944, the Japanese discovered a native resistance movement in Borneo: about 20,000 were killed ruthlessly.

People who were drafted for labor in distant regions were left to their fate when the job was done. Many of these found a miserable death. It has been estimated that out of 300,000 laborers on the East coast of Sumatra, 50 per cent have disappeared while many others are still in a poor physical condition.

After the capitulation of Java conditions in the concentration camps for Europeans became horrible beyond description, and there is no doubt that the atom bomb and the sudden collapse of Japan saved the lives of many of these unfortunate people.*

The promise of independence to the Indies was not made by the Japanese in the beginning. Tojo in the early stages merely promised "participation in government," in the form of a Central Council and Regional Councils in Java and, later on, of advisory councils in other sections of the Indies.

The Japanese divided the Indies into several administrative units, some under army and some under navy control. Java and Madoera were a unit of military administration, as well as Sumatra, although this was combined with Malaya and governed from Singapore in the beginning. Dutch Borneo and the "Great East," comprising Celebes, the Moluccas

---

* Several of the passages on the preceding pages are based upon: *Het ontstaan van de Republiek Indonesia* by T. M. A. van Loeben Sels, Gouda and Arnhem, 1946.

and the islands east of Bali were under naval administration with headquarters on Macassar.

The Java councils were hailed as a step toward self-government although they merely rubber-stamped Japanese decisions and were always attended by Japanese officials. It was only when the Japanese began to doubt the permanence of their hold on South East Asia that they began to promise "independence in the future" to the Indies. The first announcement was made in September, 1944, during the 85th session of the Diet by the Prime Minister, Kuniaki Koiso.

It was an obvious psychological move. If the Indies were given independence, propaganda could picture the arrival of the Allied armies as an "invasion" of an independent territory. This would make it possible to stir up the Indonesians to fight for the maintenance of their "independence."

This attempt of the Japanese to obtain collaboration in the form of a psychological "delayed action bomb" obviously created confusion in the Indonesian mind.

The failure of the economic side of the plans for a Greater East Asia Co-prosperity Sphere contributed much to make the Indonesians wary of the Japanese. The lack of shipping was the main cause that Japan failed to bring about an exchange of goods as planned and the resulting malnutrition and starvation turned their propaganda into hollow phrases. There was an over-abundance of articles such as rubber, sugar, tea, etc., which were world export products before the war but there was a shortage of others.

The output of a number of tropical products was curtailed which ran definitely against the interests of the Indonesians while nothing came of imports of desperately needed articles like textiles and rice. In fact, they were requisitioned by the Japanese for their own use.

Currency manipulations were another means whereby the Japanese imposed a burden upon the occupied territories. They introduced the military yen or script in addition to the original currency and began by establishing a forced rate of exchange in the same way that the Germans did.

This military script was not negotiable in Japan, while the internal yen was not valid outside Japan. The military yen was put into circulation without any return in goods or services from Japan, creating an inflationary effect.

The regions of southeast Asia were supposed to contribute one third of the budget of Greater Japan although it was not clear how this was going to be organized as most of the territories were operating under a deficit.

There is no doubt that the Indonesians realized more and more toward the end of the war that there was little to be expected from the Japanese, but they were also determined that they did not want to return to pre-war conditions although their ideas about the future were, of necessity, vague, especially as far as economic problems were concerned.

During the war years, the Indonesians were cut off from the outside world. Occasional air raids, occasional stories about reports of guerilla fighting in the outlying possessions, some news via the grapevine were the only contacts with the Allied nations.

In the meantime the Dutch were as active as possible in rebuilding their air force, their navy and whatever land forces they could scrape together.

Airmen were trained in Australia and the United States, and soon began to give a good account of themselves again.

In Ferbruary, 1944, the first reports came in about continued land fighting in New Guinea in which Dutch forces participated.

On April 22, when the Americans landed at Hollandia, in Netherlands New Guinea, things really began to move in the opposite direction. Hollandia was the first Netherlands territory to be liberated from the Japanese and had great potential military value on account of its airfield.

Together with the American forces, officers of the Netherlands East Indies Civil Administration landed in Hollandia and took immediate charge of the civil administration. They included medical, supply and distribution officials who had been trained in Australia and who had had practical experience in relief work at Merauke and other parts of southern Netherlands New Guinea, the only section of the Netherlands East Indies which remained free throughout the entire war.

Indonesian leaders from Australia, several of whom had made daring escapes from Japanese-held territory, broadcast the news of the re-cature of Hollandia to the population of the Indies. They called upon the people of the Indies to prepare the way for the Allied Armies of Liberation.

In the meantime, air attacks on Sumatra where ultimately the other prong of the Allied pincer was scheduled to close were intensified.

For weeks, fighting in the impenetrable jungles of New Guinea continued. Then, on May 19, the Allied forces, leap-frogging 125 miles westward from Hollandia, seized the Wakde area in Netherlands New Guinea. This operation threw the Japanese rear area in New Guinea, already disrupted by the seizure of Hollandia, into further confusion while possession of the Wakde air base gave adequate air coverage over all Netherlands New Guinea.

In the same period Australian and Dutch air attacks on Timor and surrounding islands grew daily in intensity. The island of Biak, in Geelvink Bay, off New Guinea, was also captured by the Allies, as well as Wakde Island, off the coast of Northern New Guinea. In this three month period, the Dutch air force dropped more than 500,000 pounds of bombs on Japanese targets, according to a statement of June 21 by Lieutenant General L. H. van Oyen, Commander-in-Chief of the Netherlands Indies Army.

Then the story of air raids and the capture of strategic islands continues. It is the process of the Japanese aggression in reverse: slower, but with infinitely more punch. Every where the Dutch civil administration found a hearty welcome: treatment of the natives by the Japs had been harsh and cruel, and civilization had not advanced in those parts to dreams of political independence.

The landing of Allied troops at Sansapoer, the northernmost point of Western New Guinea, meant the final stage in the reconquest of that territory. Disorder and confusion among the Japanese was considerable. The damaging of 191 Japanese vessels in that period had thrown their whole communications system out of gear.

Air control of the Allies soon began to reach to the Moluccas. On September 15, General MacArthur's forces landed on the Island of Morotai, the first reconquered region inhabited by Malayans and not by Papuans like New Guinea. Also here Netherlands East Indies civil government was established immediately, and succeeded in bringing in much needed supplies.

Allied air attacks now reached for the first time targets on Java, like Batavia, while the Borneo airfields came in for a heavy pounding. This happened in September, 1944, while the Allied Armies were also rolling forward victoriously through southern Holland.

On May 1, 1945, five days prior to the complete liberation of the Netherlands, Australian forces landed on Tarakan Island, off the eastern coast of Borneo. They captured the important port against embittered resistance by the Japanese. After a few days fighting, the town itself as well as the surrounding territory had been reconquered. It was not a glorious defeat for the Japanese compared with the strong resistance which the Dutch had put up in this area in 1942.

The Australians and the Netherlands Indies Civil Administration immediately organized relief for the numerous wounded and refugee Indonesians who flooded Tarakan. Slave laborers had appalling stories to tell.

A Netherlands Indies oil rehabilitation team landed on Tarakan with the Allied forces. It had enough equipment to restore the installations although this was a long and tedious job.

A number of the oil experts were Indonesian technicians who had been trained in Australia.

In the meantime, small segments of troops from the liberated Netherlands began to arrive in Australia. Recruiting centers had been set up all over Holland, but the process was slow as there was no equipment available. Whether recruiting in the south, which was liberated earlier, had been efficiently organized, later became a subject of controversy in the Netherlands.

On July 1, the Allies, consisting of Australian and some Netherlands Indies troops, started their assault on the oil center of Balikpapan. The attack was preceded by a ten day heavy bombardment. Again in this case, the work of the Netherlands Indies Civil Administration officials has been praised for efficient organization of the relief work for the population which was in pretty bad shape. Repeatedly the work was praised by American Army authorities.

"I, today, complete my first month in Netherlands territory, having spent some time on both the mainland of New Guinea and on one of the adjacent islands. I have been greatly impressed with the job your people are doing. The civil administration, which cooperates with the military at this particular base, is organizing rapidly in the wake of liberation. Schools are already in operation for the native Melanesians, the labor of setting up permanent installations is progressing rapidly, and there is an atmosphere of 'getting things done' in the air. I might also say that there are no better pilots in the area than those of the Netherlands East

Indies Air Force—whose ships operate regularly in the liberated territory."*

In this same period Netherlands and British submarines sank 15 Japanese warships, 20 large merchantmen, 51 coastal vessels, and 159 tugs and small craft.

Then, shortly after, the atomic bomb put an abrupt end to any possible continuation of Japanese resistance.

On August 19th, the "cease fire" order was issued for the Netherlands East Indies. The war in Indonesia had come to an end.

---

* From a letter by Lieutenant John L. Swift of the U.S. 15th Weather Squadron, as quoted in the Netherlands News, July 15, 1945.

CHAPTER XII

The Post War Period in Indonesia

THE SUDDEN END OF THE war in the Pacific posed
several serious problems. It is known now that long
before the end of the war, the Dutch government had requested the United States to assist in re-establishing authority
in the Netherlands East Indies. A tentative arrangement had
been made to the effect that American forces under the Command of General MacArthur would undertake that responsibility. Unfortunately this preliminary plan did not go into
effect as the British government feared that its prestige in
the East would suffer if American forces were to liberate an
area which was within the British operational sphere that
had been allotted to the army of Lord Louis Mountbatten.

When the moment of liberation arrived suddenly, the
British troops available for this task were far below the required number, and only a very small contingent of troops
was landed in the Indies.

It was the task of the British:

A. To accept the Japanese surrender in the Netherlands
East Indies.
B. To disarm the Japanese and remove them from the
Indies.
C. To secure the surrender of all war materials.
D. To liberate and repatriate prisoners of war.
E. To guarantee the safety of more than 100,000 intern-
ees, mostly women and children.

Conditions had undergone a further complication as the
Indonesian nationalists, in collaboration with the Japanese,
had hastily proclaimed independence. Soekarno and Hatta
were returning from Indo-China but had been kept ignor-

ant about the impending Japanese capitulation. When they arrived in Batavia on August 15, they could not obtain any confirmation from the Japanese authorities about the surrender. In the night of August 15, young Indonesian nationalists urged Soekarno to proclaim independence and when he and Hatta expressed the desire to postpone the matter for a few days, they were kidnapped by the hotheaded nationalists, much to the dismay of the Japanese. The Japanese hurriedly dispatched Soebardjo to the insurgents, and the two leaders returned again to Batavia. Then, on August 17, in the presence of only a very few people, the Republic Indonesia was proclaimed, probably after secret negotiations with the Japanese commander.

When the first posters proclaiming independence appeared in Batavia, they were torn down by the Japanese police which was not informed about the event. The military authorities permitted the papers to print the proclamation but demobilized the 30,000 volunteers and 70,000 *heihoes* immediately in order to prevent a coup, although many of them were reorganized in the Republican Army.

The commission for the preparation of the Republic held meetings continuously, and added six new members on August 18, several of whom had Communist leanings. A constitution was published while Soekarno became president and Hatta vice president of the Republic. It was announced that the president would be assisted by a "national committee."

The constitution states that Indonesia is a centralized republic in which the sovereignty belongs to the people and is exercised by a parliament. The president has to be a Moslem.

Then, the Republic unleashed a strong propaganda campaign.

The population was undoubtedly expecting the arrival of the Allies with friendly feelings; the internees were given all kinds of aid by the Indonesians and the Rapwi-teams which landed by parachute were received enthusiastically. The population had had more than enough of the Japanese and was eager for peace and order. Also in Sumatra, returning planters were received with open arms by the population, and, as was outlined in the previous chapter, in the reconquered areas of the Outer Provinces, relations with the population were entirely satisfactory.

The arrival of only a small contingent of Allied troops had undoubtedly a disheartening influence on the population while the remaining in control of the Japanese army did much to arouse the hitherto uncertain feelings of nationalism and racial and religious hatred which had been stirred up systematically by the Japanese. In the beginning of the war, the rather ineffective defense of Java had done much to diminish the respect of the Indonesians for the white man, and the return of the Allies with a small force did much to reaffirm the doubts which the natives unquestionably had.

The youthful elements who had been trained by the Japanese and had kept themselves in the background began to exercise a regime of terror and to make contact with the whites, a matter of utmost danger. There were deplorable attacks on the internees.

The population as a whole remained indifferent; they were more interested in food, clothing and the re-establishment of law and order than in anything else. The extremist elements which found no counterforce in the Allies and only a pretended control in the Japanese, could create all the havoc they wanted.

The Indonesian leaders were not informed about world affairs or the economic future of the Republic and could make but the vaguest political statements.

The situation became even more confused when the British commander General Sir Philip Christison started with a sort of "de facto" recognition of the insecure "republic" instead of establishing military government and postponing political considerations until a more opportune time.

It does not have to be said that these developments affected the Dutch in Holland like a thunderstroke out of a clear sky. The occupation period had created a strong psychological reaction which had made the nation proud of her record in the Indies and eager to continue with a progressive program as had been announced by the Queen in December, 1942.

The chaotic conditions in Java, the ill-treatment of women and children, the hesitant attitude of the British made people feel bitter and critical: critical of their allies, of their own government and above all of the East Indies Government. For a while Dr. H. van Mook was the best hated man in Holland, especially among former residents of the Indies who interpreted his progressive attitude as a sign of weakness.

The stream of pamphlets and the number of meetings became staggering, but an outside observer could not help noticing that five years of occupation had also left the Dutch unaware of developments in the world so that they did not give sufficient consideration to the changes which had taken place.

The strongest voices of protest came from J. W. Meyer Ranneft, former President of the People's Council, and from Professor C. Gerretson who regarded Dr. van Mook as the liquidator of the Netherlands Empire.

Especially Professor Gerretson became very extreme in his attacks and charged the Indies government with poor preparations in Australia as well as with having secretly opposed the training of recruits in the Southern Netherlands, as the Indies government insisted on training in Australia which later proved to be impossible.

It also caused bitterness in Holland that the Anglo-Saxon press seemed to favor the republicans and did not take sufficient trouble to find out how conditions actually were. It is true that in the beginning the American press took a favorable view of the independence movement, but the attacks on the internment camps as well as the realization that the Outer Provinces were by no means behind the Republic, as well as the outstanding administrative record of the Dutch, soon caused the leading newspapers to take a more objective view of the situation, and, on the whole, it can be said that the American press favors a compromise which would be fair to all parties concerned.

For a time, however, emotions were so stirred up that people in Holland were in no mood for any compromise. The more conservative elements argued that it was the first task of the Dutch to re-establish order in the Indies and that political matters should only be considered later on the basis of the promises of the Dutch government. The opposite view is taken by the Communist Party which favors Indonesian independence while the other parties support the government policy but are hoping for a compromise which would continue the tie with the Indies, especially in the economic realm.

Information about actual conditions in the Indies was as scanty as the news in the Indies about Holland. This condition did not serve to make understanding any easier. Moreover, the world in general did not realize that there was little unity in the Indonesian independence movement. Most of the Outer Provinces are opposed to Javanese domination and to the republic as it has developed so far.

When the Netherlands Parliamentary Commission, which visited the Indies, came to Macassar in South Celebes, they found that the population was not willing to go along with Java as far as breaking the tie with Holland was concerned. They were anxious to obtain self-government but within the framework of the Netherlands Kingdom as they are strongly opposed to domination by heavily populated Java. In Ambon, Timor and other parts of the Moluccas and the lesser Sunda

Islands the feeling was similar. The entire region was perfectly orderly; the island of Flores, for instance, with 500,000 inhabitants, was policed by 50 Dutch M.P.'s.

In Borneo there was a moment of unrest in November but the majority of the population has become very friendly toward the Dutch.

The birthday of Princess Juliana was celebrated by the entire population on April 30, 1946. The sultan of Western Borneo was strongly opposed to a Java-dominated republic while on Bali the relations with the Dutch troops are satisfactory.

On Sumatra the condition is utterly confused: parts are completely in the hands of the local bosses who rule as they see fit and have not much contact with Java. Japanese and English troops protect the oilfields while the Javanese plantation workers are in a deplorable condition.

The Chinese population in the Indies of about a million and a quarter is divided. As they form the middle class in the Indies, they have nothing much to gain from a republican government. Some of them are under Communist influence but the majority tries to follow a non-political attitude.

On Java itself the Republican government was powerless to prevent excesses which they undoubtedly disapproved. The attacks on Dutch men, women and children, the senseless fighting with British and Dutch army units, the attacks on Chinese, Indonesian Christians and Eurasians cannot but be considered as the outcome of Japanese propaganda which the Indonesians will ultimately regret themselves and which could have been prevented if larger military forces had been available for the Indies. However, the continued presence in the Indies of large Japanese forces undoubtedly lent courage to a number of irresponsible elements. It is also certain that Japanese officers continued to act as advisers to Soekarno although gradually the more moderate Sjahrir faction has gained in importance. Whether the influence of the Communist, Tan Malakka, who is influential in labor and farmer organizations, is waning is hard to ascertain.

Economically the entire archipelago is in a difficult position although the Outer Provinces are better off than Java. The total destruction has been estimated at 8 billion guilders. As this includes extensive productive apparatus, it is obvious that this means a serious setback for the population which can only be overcome by new capital investments. It need not be said that the Republic would hardly be considered an attractive object for foreign loans, and the Javanese leaders undoubtedly realize that collaboration with the Dutch will be essential for a return to economic progress and further economic developments. At the moment the conditions are chaotic: food as well as clothing is seriously short, and life has returned to the primitive stage of a largely local economy.

Communications, public utilities, etc., are working poorly or not at all, and the population is more than anxious for a return to normal conditions. Hospitals are beginning to deteriorate, and in many instances it is daily becoming clearer that the ties with the West cannot be severed. Another matter of great importance is that Dutch shipping is of essential value to the prosperity of Indonesia and its contacts with the entire world.

It was not until September 29, 1945, that the first British occupation troops landed in Tandjoengpriok, port of Batavia, while British naval forces assumed control of the harbor area. Proclamations were posted in the streets of Batavia which announced the defeat and surrender of the Japanese and the intention of the Allies "to maintain law and order until the government of the Netherlands Indies is once again functioning."

Lieutenant-General Sir Philip Christison, British Commander, made it also known that he intended to occupy only two cities on Java—Batavia and Soerabaja—and two on

Sumatra—Medan and Padang. In other areas, law and order would have to be maintained by the Japanese.

It caused great surprise among the Dutch when General Christison announced that he expected the "Indonesian government" to take charge of the civil administration in non-occupied areas and the Netherlands troops be excluded from the landing forces because the Soekarno government was opposed to it. He also stated that a conference would be held, but the Dutch steadfastly refused to deal with Soekarno whom they regarded as a collaborator.

The situation was aggravated by the fact that Australian dock workers refused to load ships destined for the Netherlands East Indies.

In the meantime the power of the Allies became increasingly smaller as the nationalists took large stores of arms from the Japanese and started to take over control wherever they felt strong enough to do so.

Around the middle of October when the nationalists issued a call for a "Holy war against the Dutch," the situation seemed to get out of control entirely. Killings and kidnappings were the order of the day, and little could be done to restore order.

Especially the situation of the internees in Middle Java became serious as they were menaced by attacks as well as by the outbreak of diseases.

The situation eased a little when it was announced on October 26 that the Netherlands Indies officials and a five-man delegation representing the "Indonesian Republic" planned to meet with General Christison to discuss the situation. There seemed to be a feeling among the nationalists by that time that in the discussions with the Netherlands, Soekarno should be replaced by a "Republican" official more acceptable to the Dutch.

Matters came to a standstill again when severe fighting broke out in the Soerabaja area which culminated in the murder of the British Brigadier-General A. W. S. Mallaby while discussing details of the cease-fire order. Additional troops were rushed to Java as the British realized that the time had come to get "tough."

In Batavia, in the meantime, talks had finally started, although no announcements were made about the contents or results of the talks. While the talks as well as the fighting, especially in the Soerabaja area, continued, a new cabinet was formed under Sutan Sjahrir as Prime Minister.

Sjahrir has always been reputed to be more moderate than Soekarno, and he is definitely more Western in his views. He is regarded as a socialist although not of a pronounced Marxian type. Sjahrir's first act was to promise to put an end to the existing conditions of violence and to study the relations with the Netherlands at the earliest opportunity.

There were signs of dissension among the extremists' wing of the nationalists who ignored Sjahrir's pleas for moderation and continued to proclaim an all-out war against the British and the Dutch. While the heavy fighting in the Soerabaja area and intermittently in Central Java and Batavia continued, Dr. van Mook and Sutan Sjahrir began a series of conferences which, in the beginning, led to little or no results.

The increasing anarchy and lawlessness which resulted in the most wanton acts of cruelty caused a firmer attitude on the part of the British and the realization that the esablishment of law and order was absolutely imperative. Throughout December fighting continued in the Soerabaja, Bandoeng and Ambarawa sections; attempts to end the strife were continually upset by the actions of youthful extremist elements.

In the beginning of 1946, when the situation on Java and Sumatra was showing some slight improvement, the Netherlands government made a statement on its policy in regard to Indonesia.

". . . The Netherlands government consequently [on the basis of the Queen's statement of December 6, 1942. *Author's note*] take the view that the people of Indonesia should, after a given preparatory period, be enabled freely to decide their political destiny; therefore, the Netherlands government, deeply conscious of their responsibility, consider it their duty to do everything in their power in order to create and to fulfill as soon as possible the conditions which will permit such a free decision to be taken and which will assure its international recognition, thereby complying with Article 73 of the United Nations Charter.

"Without deviating in any way from the above-mentioned principle the Netherlands government are furthermore convinced that the true interests of the country and of the respective peoples of Indonesia will thereafter also find their best guarantee in the voluntary continuation, in the words of her Majesty, of: 'One realm in which the Netherlands, Indonesia, Surinam and Curacao will participate with complete self-reliance and freedom of conduct for each part regarding its internal affairs but with the readiness to render mutual assistance.'

"The Netherlands government therefore intend, in consultation with authoritative representatives of Indonesia selected from a large variety of groups, to draft a structure for the Kingdom and for Indonesia based upon democratic partnership. This structure will remain in force for a given period of time, during which it is believed that the conditions which will make possible the taking of the above-mentioned free decision will be fulfilled; after that period the partners shall independently decide upon the continuance of their relations of a then complete and voluntary partnership. Difference of opinion regarding the question whether that period should be further extended before a free decision

can be taken shall be submitted to a procedure of concilia-
tion or, if necessary, of arbitration.

"With respect to the structure mentioned in the foregoing
paragraph, discussion will be held in accordance with the
following main points:

"A. There shall be a Commonwealth of Indonesia, a part-
ner in the Kingdom composed of territories possessing different degrees of autonomy.

"B. There shall be established an Indonesian citizenship
for all born in Indonesia; Netherlands and Indonesian citizens shall be entitled to exercise all civic rights in all parts of
the Kingdom.

"C. The domestic affairs of the Commonwealth of Indonesia shall be managed independently by the Commonwealth's own institutions: for the Commonwealth as a whole
the creation of a democratic representative body containing therefore a substantial Indonesian majority is contemplated and furthermore a Cabinet formed in political har-
mony with the representative body and a representative of
the Crown as the head of the Government's executive.

"F. The central institutions functioning for the entire
Kingdom shall be composed of representatives of the con-
stituent parts of the Kingdom. The establishment of a
Commonwealth Cabinet composed of Ministers from the
constituent parts of the Kingdom is contemplated as is also
Commonwealth legislation requiring the agreement of the
Parliaments of the respective constituent parts of the
Kingdom.

"G. After the entry into force of the above-mentioned
Constitution the Netherlands government shall promote the
early admission of the Commonwealth of Indonesia as a member of the United Nations organization."

These proposals were handed to Sutan while Minister of
Overseas Territories, J. H. A. Logemann, broadcast an ex-

planation to the Netherlands people. These suggestions cleared the atmosphere so far that the Indonesian delegation decided to come to the Netherlands to continue the discussions there. From April 9 to 25 a conference was held at St. Hubertus Lodge, a modern country estate in the center of Holland. The main point of discussion was that the Dutch visualized Indonesian autonomy within the framework of the Dutch commonwealth while the Indonesian delegation was in favor of the constitution of the "Republic Indonesia" as a sovereign state which would then form a firm political and economic alliance with the Netherlands. Some headway on this point was made by considering the preliminary arrangement concluded between the French Republic and the Viet Nam. This arrangement is based on the principle that Viet Nam will form as an "état libre" part of the "Federation Indo-Chinoise" and consequently of the "Union Francaise." The application of a similar arrangement to the Indies would lead to the conclusion that the Indonesian Republic could become a part of a Federal Commonwealth which could be acceptable to the nationalists as well as to the more moderate desires of the Outer Provinces.

It was undoubtedly realized in the Netherlands that the Republic, in spite of its "vitium originis" had acquired a hold on the imagination of the population and would not be abandoned anymore. The nationalists also feel that, in principle, they have a claim on the whole of Indonesia but they realize that their authority is limited *de facto* and they are willing to be satisfied with the status they desire within the Indonesian realm. The solution is also attractive to the Netherlands as the tie with the Netherlands would be maintained on a free basis.

"The Government is of the opinion that this conception [of the republic Java as a constituent part of an Indonesian federation. *Author's note*] may be acceptable indeed insofar as Java is concerned. It does not overlook the fact that many objections may be raised to the Republic in its present original form, and that these objections do not exist only in government circles nor only among Dutchmen here and in the Indies, but just as much among Indonesians. On the other hand, it feels certain that the group which is now governing the Republic, although not at all without opposition, is regarded as being representative of the national aim also by those Indonesians in Java who, for some reason or other, would have nothing to do with the Republic. This has been expressed even by Mr. Slamet whose loyalty to the Kingdom is unquestionable. One of these reasons, the principal one, is that the Republic, as the exponent of the revolution, will automatically disappear as soon as this organization as such gives up its revolutionary attitude by recognizing the sovereignty of the Crown."

On the basis of these considerations, it was decided to hold discussions with representatives of the Outer Provinces in an effort to create autonomous organs for those regions while the conversations with the Republican leaders continued in order to iron out a number of difficulties. The Republican leaders continued to insist upon recognition of a *de facto* government of Java and Sumatra which would enter into an alliance with the Netherlands. The Republicans wanted representatives of the Outer Provinces to participate in the negotiations about the creation of an Indonesian Free State; a special relationship would be established for those territories which objected to unconditional inclusion while a plebescite would be held after three years to decide on this relationship. The proposals of Sjahrir also included the restriction of the further entry of Netherlands troops.

This attitude led again to a deadlock of the negotiations as it went beyond the previously foreseen solution of a kind of commonwealth arrangement.

A step forward was taken with the Malino Conference which was opened on July 16 by Acting Governor General Dr. H. J. van Mook and which was attended by representatives of all the Outer Provinces.

The conference was destined to appoint delegates to the forthcoming Conference of the Realm as well as to discuss the status of the regions represented. Of fourteen speakers who made their opinions heard on July 1, eight favored maximum autonomy within the framework of the Kingdom, four supported cooperation with the Republicans of Java and Sumatra, one advocated that full freedom be granted to Indonesia after which maximum cooperation with the Netherlands would be arranged, while one delegate asked for an inter-island plebescite to decide the issue.

When Dr. van Mook summarized the views of the conference, he said:

". . . The second point on which practically all the delegates expressed their conviction is that cooperation between the Netherlands and Indonesia is necessary, and, yes, desirable. This is not only based on ages-old relations but also on positive appreciation of what Netherlands help has meant in the past, while realizing that Holland is not and cannot be an imperial power.

"The third general opinion is the desirability on the one hand of retaining the cohesion created by history and, on the other hand, of realizing such cohesion in a federative system, an Indonesian federation or a United States of Indonesia. There is equally unanimous agreement that it is desirable to establish as soon as possible a representative body with legislative powers for the entire area."

The conference adopted unanimously resolutions recommending establishment of a federated "United States of Indonesia," composed of four states Java, Sumatra, Borneo and the "Great East" (the islands east of Borneo and Java).

The transition period which would elapse before the relationship with the Netherlands would be finally determined, was set at a period of five or ten years while some held the view that the Conference of the Realm should define the duration of the transition period. The matter of collaboration after the treaty period was seen either within the framework of the Netherlands Kingdom or guaranteed by a bilateral treaty.

In reality, conditions in the Outer Provinces were also proceeding very satisfactorily, and, on July 15 martial law was lifted for the entire archipelago except Java and Sumatra.

To make progress smoother, a Commission-General for the Netherlands Indies was instituted on August 3 by the Netherlands government. It was established to form continual, daily contact between the Netherlands government in the Hague and the Netherlands Indies government in Batavia in order (1) to eliminate restrictions now imposed on Netherlands Sovereignty in the Indies and promote discussions to this end with British authorities; (2) to determine the share that the Netherlands, and possibly, foreign powers would have in the financial and economic reconstruction of the Indies; (3) to regulate the task of Dutch forces in the restoration of law and order in the Indies; (4) to care for Dutch troops in the Indies; (5) to supervise repatriation; (6) to restore Netherlands culture and education which the Japanese destroyed systematically after the occupation.

The main task of the Commission consists of the preparation of the new political organization for the Indies, and, in consequence thereof, the forthcoming Conference of the Realm.

Negotiations were resumed again on August 20 after they had been interrupted by an abortive coup d'état against Soekarno and the kidnapping of Sjahrir by extremists elements. In the meantime, the gradual replacement of British troops by Dutch forces proceeded satisfactorily, and it was estimated that toward the end of the year the British would have left and that 40,000-50,000 Dutch troops would be available to maintain order.

A great step forward was taken when Sjahrir proposed a Dutch-Indonesian truce while the evacuation of Allied interees from the interior was again resumed. As life was beginning to be somewhat more normal in the Indies, Dr. van Mook decided to call a second conference at Pangkalpinang, Bali, of representatives of the Outer Provinces in view of the great success of the Malino Conference.

The fact that matters proceeded so smoothly in the Outer Provinces and that life there had swung back to normal had an undoubtedly sobering effect on the Javanese nationalists who were still facing chaotic conditions in the regions which they controlled.

When the discussions on Java, with the new Commission-General, under the chairmanship of former Premier, Willem Schermerhorn, started again, they took place in a much improved atmosphere. Distrust and tension on both sides had diminished considerably, and Dutch as well as Indonesians were convinced of the sincerity of one another's intentions.

The culmination of these trends came when on October 14 a truce in military activities between Allied and Indonesian armed forces was concluded, and real peace had finally come to the Indies. With it will come the realization that all parts of the Indies population, the Indonesians, the Dutch, the Chinese and the Arabs, have contributed to the development of that rich and beautiful territory, and that further progress will come from realistic collaboration between the same groups. When peace and order reign once more, the Indonesians themselves will realize that a strong tie with the West is essential for them to reach their goal of a prosperous and harmonious community, and that the Netherlands, as an economically active but non-imperialistic country, is one of the natural contact points, a contact that over a period of three centuries has brought peace and order to the Indies in spite of a number of shortcomings which the Dutch themselves realize were inherent in a system they intend to improve in their own country as well. In a more united world, Dutch-Indonesian friendship cannot but contribute a constructive element which will be free on both sides of excessive self-interest.

* * * * *

THE END

On November 15th, an agreement was signed whereby the United States of Indonesia will remain an integral part of the Netherlands Kingdom. The text of the agreement is given in the Appendix.

Appendix

TEXT OF THE DUTCH-INDONESIAN AGREEMENT

Batavia, Java, Nov. 18 (Aneta) — The text of the draft agreement between the Netherlands and the Republic of Indonesia, as published here today:

PREAMBLE

The Netherlands Government, represented by the Commission General for the Netherlands Indies, and the Government of the Republic of Indonesia, represented by the Indonesian delegation, moved by a sincere desire to insure good relations between the peoples of the Netherlands and Indonesia in new forms of voluntary cooperation which offer the best guarantee for sound and strong development of both countries in the future and which make it possible to give a new foundation to the relationship between the two peoples, agree as follows and will submit this agreement at the shortest possible notice for the approval of the respective parliaments:

ARTICLE I

The Netherlands Government recognizes the Government of the Republic of Indonesia as exercising de facto authority over Java, Madura and Sumatra. The areas occupied by Allied or Netherlands forces shall be included gradually, through mutual cooperation, in republican territory. To this end, the necessary measures shall at once be taken in order that this inclusion shall be completed at the latest on the date mentioned in Article XII.

ARTICLE II

The Netherlands Government and the Government of the Republic shall cooperate in the rapid formation of a sovereign democratic state on a federal basis to be called the United States of Indonesia.

ARTICLE III

The United States of Indonesia shall comprise the entire territory of the Netherlands Indies, with the provision, however, that in case the population of any territory, after due consultation with the other territories, should decide by democratic process that they are not, or not yet, willing to join the United States of Indonesia, they can establish a special relationship for such a territory to the United States of Indonesia and to the Kingdom of the Netherlands.

ARTICLE IV

The component parts of the United States of Indonesia shall be the Republic of Indonesia, Borneo and the Great East without prejudice to the right of the population of any territory to decide by democratic process that its position in the United States of Indonesia shall be arranged otherwise. Without derogation of the provisions of Article III and of the first paragraph of this article, the United States of Indonesia may make special arrangements concerning the territory of its capital.

ARTICLE V

The Constitution of the United States of Indonesia shall be determined by a Constituent Assembly composed of the democratically nominated representatives of the Republic and of the other future partners of the United States of Indonesia to which the following paragraph of this article shall apply. Both parties shall consult each other on the method of participation in this Constituent Assembly by the Republic of Indonesia, by the territories not under the authority of the Republic and by the groups of the population not, or insufficiently, represented with due observance of the responsibility of the Netherlands Government and the Government of the Republic, respectively.

ARTICLE VI

To promote the joint interests of the Netherlands and Indonesia, the Netherlands Government and the Government of the Republic of Indonesia shall cooperate in the establishment of a Netherlands-Indonesian Union by which the Kingdom of the Netherlands, comprising the Netherlands, the Netherlands Indies, Surinam and Curacao, shall be converted into said union consisting on the one hand of the Kingdom of the Netherlands, comprising the Netherlands, Surinam and Curacao, and on the other hand the United States of Indonesia.

The foregoing paragraph does not exclude the possibility of a further arrangement of the relations between the Netherlands, Surinam and Curacao.

ARTICLE VII

(A) The Netherlands-Indonesian Union shall have its own organs to promote the joint interests of the Kingdom of the Netherlands and the United States of Indonesia.

(B) These organs shall be formed by the Governments of the Kingdom of the Netherlands and the United States of Indonesia, and, if necessary, by the Parliaments of those countries.

(C) The joint interests shall be considered to be cooperation on foreign relations, defense and, as far as necessary, finance, as well as subjects of an economic or cultural nature.

ARTICLE VIII

The King (Queen) of the Netherlands shall be at the head of the Netherlands-Indonesian Union. Decrees and resolutions concerning the joint interests shall be issued by the organs of the union in King's (Queen's) name.

ARTICLE IX

In order to promote the interests of the United States of Indonesia in the Netherlands and the Kingdom of the Netherlands in Indonesia, a High Commissioner shall be appointed by the respective Governments.

ARTICLE X

Statutes of the Netherlands-Indonesian Union, shall, furthermore, contain provisions regarding:

(A) Safeguarding of the rights of both parties toward one another and guarantees for the fulfillment of their mutual obligations;

(B) Mutual exercise of civic rights by Netherlands and Indonesian citizens;

(C) Regulations containing provisions in case no agreement can be reached by the organs of the union;

(D) Regulation of the manner and conditions of the assistance to be given by the services of the Kingdom of the Netherlands to the United States of Indonesia as long as the services of the latter are not, or are insufficiently, organized; and

(E) Safeguarding in both parts of the Union of the fundamental human rights and liberties referred to in the Charter of the United Nations' organization.

ARTICLE XI

(A) The statutes of the Netherlands-Indonesian Union shall be drafted by a conference of the representatives of the Kingdom of the Netherlands and the future United States of Indonesia.

(B) The statutes shall come into effect after approval by the respective parliaments.

ARTICLE XII

The Netherlands Government and the Government of the Republic of Indonesia shall endeavor to establish the United States of Indonesia and the Netherlands-Indonesian Union before Jan. 1, 1949.

ARTICLE XIII

The Netherlands Government shall forthwith take the necessary steps in order to obtain the admission of the United States of Indonesia as a member of the United Nations' organization immediately after the formation of the Netherlands-Indonesian Union.

ARTICLE XIV

The Government of the Republic of Indonesia recognizes the claims of all non-Indonesians to the restoration of their rights and the restitution of their goods as far as they are exercised or to be found in the territory over which it exercises de facto authority. A joint commission will be set up to effect this restoration and restitution.

ARTICLE XV

In order to reform the Government of the Indies in such a way that its composition and procedure shall conform as closely as possible to the recognition of the Republic of Indonesia and to its projected constitutional structure, the Netherlands Government, pending the realization of the United States of Indonesia and of the Netherlands-Indonesian Union, shall forthwith initiate the necessary legal measures to adjust the constitutional and international position of the Kingdom of the Netherlands to the new situation.

ARTICLE XVI

Directly after the conclusion of this agreement, both parties shall proceed to reduce their armed forces. They will consult together concerning the extent and rate of this reduction and their cooperation in military matters.

ARTICLE XVII

(A) For the cooperation between the Netherlands Government and the Government of the Republic contemplated in this agreement, an organization shall be called into existence consisting of delegations to be appointed by each of the two Governments with a joint secretariat.

(B) The Netherlands Government and the Government of the Republic of Indonesia shall settle by arbitration any dispute which might arise from this agreement and which cannot be solved by joint consultation in conference between those delegations. In that case a chairman of another nationality with a deciding vote shall be appointed by agreement between the delegations or, if such agreement cannot be reached, by the President of the International Court of Justice.

ARTICLE XVIII

This agreement shall be drawn up in the Netherlands and Indonesian languages. Both texts shall have equal authority.

Bibliography

ADAMIC, L. *A nation of nations,* New York, 1945.

ADAMSON, H. C. *Lands of new world neighbors,* New York, 1941.

AKEN, N. van. *The economic dependence of America on the products of Netherlands India,* New York, 1934.

AMERICAN ACADEMY OF POLITICAL AND SOCIAL SCIENCE. *The Netherlands during German occupation,* Philadelphia, 1946.

AMSTERDAM, HAVENDIENST. *One year free: Sea and Rhine port of Amsterdam,* Amsterdam, 1946.

ARNDT, C. O. *International educational relations,* New York, 1946.

ASHTON, H. S. *The Netherlands at war,* London, 1941.

BAKKER, P. *Pauperiseeren, emigreeren, vegeteeren of annexeeren,* Amsterdam, 1945.

BALEN, W. J. van. *Ons gebiedsdeel Curacao,* Haarlem, 1938.
——*The territory of Curacao,* Amsterdam, 1939.

BALLINTIJN, G. *Data, feiten, documenten,* Enschede, 1945.

BARNOUW, A. J. *Cross currents of culture in Indonesia,* 1946.
——*The Dutch,* New York, 1940.
——*Holland under Queen Wilhelmina,* New York, 1923.
——*The land of William of Orange,* New York, 1944.
——*The making of modern Holland,* New York, 1944.

BARNOUW, A. J. and LANDHEER, B. Eds. *The contribution of Holland to the sciences,* New York, 1943.

BARTH, M. P. *Organisatie v. h. bedrijfsleven,* Amsterdam, 1945.

BEELAERTS VAN BLOKLAND, F. *The five days of Holland,* Washington, 1940.

BEERS, A. C. VAN.*Holanda,* New York, 1944.
——*Periscoop op,* London, 1945.
——*Queen Wilhelmina's country,* London, 1943.

BERGSMA, A. J. *Maatschappelijke verhoudingen,* Arnhem, 1945.

BEUS, J C. DE (BOISOT, pseud).) *Wedergeboorte v. h. Koninkrijk,* London, 1943.

BEUKERS, F. M. *What nu?* Schiedam, 1945.

BISSON, T. A. *The Netherlands Indies at war,* New York, 1941.

BLOK, P. J. *History of the people of the Netherlands,* New York, 1898-1900.

BLOKDIJK, W. *Ons politieke leven.* Utrecht, 1945.

BOAS, J. H. *Resistance of the churches in the Netherlands,* New York, 1944.

BOEKE, J. H. *The structure of Netherlands Indian economy,* New York, 1942.

BOER, D. W. N. DE. *Wat iedereen weten moet met betrekking tot "Het Indonesische probleem,"* 's—Gravenhage, 1946.

BOISOT, *pseud. see* BEUS, J. D. DE.

BOLKESTEIN, G. *Religious and cultural resistance in the Netherlands,* Havana, 1944.

BOND VAN ANTI-ANNEXATIE-COMITE'S. *Rapport over het annexatie-vraagstuk, Alphen a. d.* Rijn, 1926.

BOOLEN, J J. *Five years of occupation, The Netherlands,* D.A.V.I.D., 1945.

BOOY, A. F. DE. *Waarom wij zullen winnen,* Willemstad, 1940.

BOUSQUET, G. H. *A French view of the Netherlands Indies,* London, 1940.

BOVENE, G. A. VAN. *Hier is Indië!* Utrecht, 1939.
——*Nieuws!* Batavia, 1941.
——*Wij varen voort,* Batavia, 1941.

BRAAKE, A. L. TER. *Mining in the Netherlands East Indies,* New York, 1944.

BRINK, J. R. M. VAN DEN. *Eenige economische aspecten v. h. vraagstuk der herstelbetalingen,* Nijmegen, 1945.

BRIX, W J. G. *Waarom moeten Nederland en Oost-Indië een zijn?* Deventer, 1945.

BROEK, J. VAN DEN. *Annexatie van Duitsch grondgebied ter compensatie van door Nederland geleden schade,* Utrecht, 1945.

BROEK, J. O. M. *Diversity and unity in Southeast Asia,* New York, 1944.
——*Economic development of the Netherlands Indies,* New York, 1942.
——*The economic development of the outer provinces of the Netherlands Indies,* New York, 1940.
——*Indonesia and the Netherlands,* New York, 1943.

BROMBERG, P. *Architecture in the Netherlands,* New York, 1944.
——*Decorative arts in the Netherlands,* New York, 1944.
——*Doelmatig bouwen en wonen,* New York, 1945.

BROUWER, H. A. *Geological expedition of the University of Amsterdam to the Lesser Sunda islands,* Amsterdam, 1940-1942.

BUIJS, D. *Wij en ons leger,* 1945.

BURGGRAAFF, W. *Voor God en vaderland,* New York, 1944.

BYVANK, A. W. *Nederland in den Romeinschen tijd,* Leiden, 1943-1945.
——*Voorgeschiedenis van Nederland,* Leiden, 1942.

CAMPEN, J. PH. M. VAN. *Onderneming en rechtsvorm*, Nijmegen, 1945.

CAPEK, K. *Letters from Holland*, London, 1933.

CARPENTER, F. *The Pacific, its lands and peoples*, New York, 1944.

CASTILOO, J. V. *Holanda y la guerra*, Bogotá, 1943.

CATOR, W. J. *The economic position of the Chinese in the Netherlands Indies*, Chicago, 1936.

CLARK, E. A. *Peoples of the China seas*, St. Louis, 1942.

CLARK, G. N. *Holland and the war*, Oxford, 1941.

CLUNE, F. *To the isles of spice*, London, 1941.

COASTAL COMMAND, *London*, Landsdrukkerij, 1943.

COENEN TORCHIANA, H. A. VAN. *Holland*, San Francisco, 1915.
——*Tropical Holland*, Chicago, 1921.

COLE, F. C. *The people of Malaysia*, New York, 1945.

COLENBRANDER, H. T. *Koloniale geschiedenis*, 's—Gravenhage, 1925.

COLIJN, H. ed. *Neerlands Indië: land en volk*, Amsterdam, 1913.

CONFERENCE OF THE INTERNATIONAL LABOUR ORGANI-ZATION, *Philadelphia, April 20-May 12*, 1944. *Verslag door de Delegatie van het Koninkrijk der Nederlanden*, New York, 1944.

COOLHAAS, W. PH. *Insulinde: Mensch en maatschappij*, Amsterdam, 1939.

COURT, J. F. H. A. DE LA. *Paedagogische richtlijnen voor Indonesië*, Deventer, 1945.
——*Het vraagstuk Indonesië*, Deventer, 1945.

DALSEN, W. J. VAN. *The Netherlands in the East*, Pretoria, 1946.

DANIEL, H. *Islands of the East Indies*, New York, 1944.
——*Islands of the Pacific*, New York, 1943.

DAT IK ZAL WEDERKEEREN, New York, 1942.

DAUKES, W. H. *The "P. & T." lands*, Batavia, 1943.

DIETRICH, E. B. *Far eastern trade of the United States*, New York, 1940.

DISCUSSION CONFERENCE ON POSTWAR PROBLEMS OF THE NETHERLANDS, Boston, 1943.

DIT VROEG INDIE, 's—Gravenhage, 1945.

DJAJADININGRAT, R. L. *Educational developments in the Netherlands Indies*, New York, 1942.
——*From illiteracy to university*, New York, 1943.

DJOJOHADIKOESOEMO, R. M. M. *Tien jaren cooperatie-voorlich-ting vanwege de overheid*, 1930-1940, Batavia, 1941.

DOOLARD, A. DEN. *Walcheren komt boven water*, Amsterdam, 1946.

DOORMAN, P. L. G. *Military operations in the Netherlands from 10th-17th May*, 1940, London, 1944.

DRIESSEN, L. A. *The history of the textile crafts in Holland*, Basle, 1944.

HET DUITSCHE AANBOD TOT EEN BEEINDIGING DER FEIT-ELIJKE VIJANDELIJKHEDEN IN HET NOG BEZETTE NED-ERLANDSCHE GEBIED VAN APRIL 1945, 's—Gravenhage, Landsdrukkerij, 1946.

DUSEN, H. P. VAN. *East Indies discoveries*, New York, 1944.

DUYVENDAK, J. PH. *Inleiding tot de ethnologie van de Indische archipel*, Groningen, 1940.

EAST INDIES INSTITUTE OF AMERICA, New York. *A list of lectures on Southeast Asia*, New York, 1945.

EENIGE HOOFDPUNTEN V. H. REGEERINGSBELEID IN LON-DON, 's—Gravenhage, Rijksuitgeverij, 1946.

EERDE, J. C. VAN. *Inleiding tot de volkenkunde van Nederlansch-Indië*, New York, 1943.

——*De volken van Nederlandsch-Indië*, New York, 1943.

ELZINGA, S. *Grondslagen voor een gelouterde democratie*, Wassenaar, 1945.

EMERSON, R. *Joint author. Government and nationalism in Southeast Asia.*

——*Malaysia, a study in direct and indirect rule*, New York, 1937.

——*The Netherlands Indies and the United States*, Boston, 1942

ENGELBERTINK, B. A. A. *Onze oostgrens*, Oldenzaal, 1945.

ENGERS, J. F. *Indië in de branding*, New York, 1945.

ESKES, T. J. *Annexatie van Duitsch grondgebied door Nederland.*

EYKEL, R. N. M., ed. *Nederland's wil en werk*, Utrecht, 1940.

FABIAN SOCIETY, London. *Dutch state coal mines*, London, 1945.

FAIRCHILD, D. *Garden islands of the Great East*, New York, 1943.

——*The world was my garden*, New York, 1944.

FISHER, H. TH. *Zending en volksleven in Nederlands-Indië*, Zwolle, 1932.

FRANKS, H. G. *Holland afloat*, London, 1942.

FULL RECORD OF THE VISIT OF H. M. QUEEN WILHELMINA TO CANADA AND THE UNITED STATES, JUNE 18th-AUGUST 26th, 1942, London, 1942.

FURNIVALL, J. S. *Educational progress in Southeast Asia,* New York, 1943.
——*Netherlands India,* New York, 1944.
GALEN, L. C. E. VAN. *Annexation of German territory incumbent upon Holland,* Amsterdam, 1945.
GELDEREN, J. VAN. *The recent development of economic foreign policy in the Netherlands East Indies,* London, 1939.
GENT, W. J. M. VAN. *Nederlandsche Katholieken en het vraagstuk eener nieuwe partijgroepeering, 's*—Hertogenbosch, 1945.
THE GERMAN EXPLOITATION OF THE NETHERLANDS IN FIGURES AND FACTS, The Hague, Min. of Commerce and Industry, 1946.
GERRETSON, C. *Coens eerherstel,* Amsterdam, 1944.
——*Indië onder dictatuur,* Amsterdam, 1946.
GEYL, P. *Nederlands-Belgische betrekkingen,* Antwerpen, 1936.
GOES VAN NATERS, M. VAN DER. *Leiding van den staat,* Haarlem, 1945.
GORDON, D. *Knowing the Netherlands,* New York, 1940.
GORTER, S. DE. *La Hollande,* London, 1944.
GRAEFF, A. C. D. ed. *Van vriend tot vijand,* Amsterdam, 1945.
GREIDANUS, TJ. *Toekomst van den gulden,* Amsterdam, 1946.
GRISWOLD, A. W. *Far Eastern policy of the United States,* New York, 1938.
HAAN, J. R. *De agrarische noodzaak van grenscorrectie,* Oostwold, 1945.
HAAR, B. TER. *Beginselen en stelsel van het adatrecht,* New York, 1943.
HAAS, J. A. DE. *Our allies,* New York, 1942.
——*Postwar reconstruction of the Netherlands,* New York, 1943.
THE HAGUE, compiled to the order of the municipality of the Hague, The Hague, 1939.
EEN HALF JAAR VRIJHEID, The Hague, Regeeringsvoorlichtingsdienst, 1945.
HALL, C. J. J. VAN. *Insulinde,* Deventer, 1939.
HAMEL, J. A. VAN. *Nederland tusschen de mogendheden,* Amsterdam, 1918.
——*Vaste koers (voor Neerlands schip van staat)* Amsterdam, 1945.
HANDBOOK OF THE NETHERLANDS AND OVERSEAS TERRITORIES, The Hague, Department of Foreign Affairs, 1931.
HANDVEST VAN DE VRIJHEID, London, Voorlichtingsdienst der Nederlandsche regeering, 1943.

HART, G. H. C. *The Netherlands Indies and their neighbors in the southwest Pacific,* New York, 1942.
——*Recent development in the Netherlands Indies,* New York, 1942.
——*Ties and barriers in the Pacific,* Ottawa, 1943.
——*Towards economic democracy in the Netherlands Indies,* New York, 1942.

HAUSERMAN, K. *Some aspects of Japan's co-prosperity sphere,* Melbourne, 1945.

HEIJST, H. VAN. *Geleide economie,* Purmerend, 1945.

HEINE-GELDERN, R. *Prehistoric research in the Netherlands Indies,* New York, 1945.
——*Research on Southeast Asia,* New York, 1946.
——*Survey of studies on Southeast Asia at American universities and colleges,* New York, 1943.

HELSDINGEN, W. H. VAN. comp. *Daar werd groots verricht,* Amsterdam, 1941.
——comp. *Mission interrupted,* Amsterdam, 1945.
——*De plaats van Nederlandsch-Indië,* Leiden, 1946.

HERMANS, H. *Parlementaire Geschiedenis van jaar tot jaar 1938-1939,* Hilversum, 1939.

HETTINGA, S. *"Repoeblik Indonesia," drieërlei houding,* Leiden, 1946.

HEUVEN GOEDHART, G. J. *Over het nieuwe Nederland,* Utrecht, 1945.

HILTERMANN, G. B. J. *Land om land,* Amsterdam, 1945.

HISS, P. H. *Bali,* New York, 1941.
——*Netherlands America,* New York, 1943.
——*A selective guide to the English literature on the Netherlands West Indies,* New York, 1943.

HOEBEL, E. A., ed. *Netherlands East and West Indies,* New York, 1945.

HOLLAND AHEAD, The Hague, Regeeringsvoorlichtingsdienst, 1946.

HOLLAND CARRIES ON: THE NETHERLANDS, New York, 1941.

HOLLAND CARRIES ON: THE NETHERLANDS EAST INDIES, New York, 1942.

HOLLAND CARRIES ON: THE NETHERLANDS WEST INDIES, New York, 1943.

HOLLAND IN DER SCHWEIZER PRESSE, Zurich, 1945.

HOLLAND IN TIMES OF WAR, Amsterdam, 1946.

HONIG, P. ed. *Science and scientists in the Netherlands Indies,* New York, 1945.

HOPKINS, A. G. *Netherlands Indies tariffs and trade controls*, New York, 1945.

HOUTEN, J. N. VAN DEN. *Bondsstaat en souvereiniteit*, Leiden, 1945.

HOW TO END THE GERMAN MENACE, New York, 1944.

HUIZINGA, J. *Geschonden wereld*, Haarlem, 1945.
——*Hoe bepaalt de geschiedenis het heden*, Haarlem, 1946.
——*In the shadow of tomorrow*, New York, 1936.
——*Nederland's geestesmerk*, Leiden, 1935.
——*Patriotisme en nationalisme in de Europeesche geschiedenis tot het einde der 19e eeuw*, Haarlem, 1940.

HUIZINGA, L. *Zes kaarsen voor Indie*, Amsterdam, 1945.

HUFFEL, A. J. VAN. *Nederlandsche schrijvers in vertaling*, Leiden, 1939.

HUFFNAGEL, G. E. *Op weg naar geleide economie*, Utrecht, 1945.

HYDRICK, J. L. *Intensive rural hygiene work in the Netherlands East Indies*, New York, 1942.

HYMA, A. *The Dutch in the Far East*, Ann Arbor, 1942.
——*An outline of the growth of Far Eastern civilizations*, Columbus, Ohio, 1946.

ILLEGALE PERS OVER NA-OORLOGSCHE PROBLEMEN, Assen, 1945.

INDONESIE IN HET PARLEMENT MEI 1946, 's—Gravenhage, Algemeene landsdrukkerij, 1946.

INDONESIE'S TOEKOMST, Batavia, Regeeringsvoorlichtingsdienst, 1946.

INDUSTRIALIZATION A VITAL ISSUE, Amsterdam, Rotterdamsche bankvereeniging, 1946.

JONG, E. VAN ZIJL DE. *The Netherlands East Indies and Japan*, New York, 1942.

JONG, L. DE. *Holland fights the Nazis*, London, 1941.
——*Je maintiendrai*, London, 1941-1945.

JONG, L. DE and STOPPELMAN, J. W. F. *The lion rampant*, New York, 1943.

JONG, S. H. *Schets van den Nederlandschen landbouw*, Utrecht, 1943.

JOSSELIN DE JONG, J. P. B. DE. *Het Indië van Meijer Ranneft*, Leiden, 1945.

KARIG, W. *Battle report*, New York, 1944.

KAT ANGELINO, A. D. A. DE. *Colonial policy*, Chicago, 1931.
——*Japan's imperialisme en zijn expansie*, Amsterdam, 1945.
KAT ANGELINO, P. DE. *Some remarks on the wages paid in the Netherlands Indies*, Batavia, 1936.
KATHOLIEKE VOLKSPARTIJ, THE HAGUE. *Urgency program of the Catholic people's party*, The Hague, Secretariat general, 1946.
KEESING, F. M. *Native peoples of the Pacific world*, New York, 1946.
KEESING, M. M. *Pacific islands in war and peace*, New York, 1944.
KENNEDY, R. *The ageless Indies*, New York, 1942.
——*Islands and peoples of the Indies*, Washington, 1943.
——*Races and peoples of the Indies*, Los Angeles, 1943.
KERNKAMP, W. J. A. *Government and Islam in the Netherlands East Indies*, New York, 1944.
KERSTENS, P. A. *Luctor et emergo*, New York, 1943.
KESSEN, A. *Het vraagstuk der annexatie*, Maastricht, 1945.'
KEUNING, H. J. *Nederlandsch-Duitsche grenslanden*, Amsterdam, 1945.
KLEFFENS, E. N. VAN. *The democratic future of the Netherlands Indies*, New York, 1942. Reprint from Foreign Affairs.
——*The foreign policy of the Netherlands*, New York, 1944.
——*If the Nazis flood Holland*, New York, 1944. Reprint from Foreign Affairs.
——*Juggernaut over Holland*, New York, 1941.
——*De overweldiging van Nederland*, London, 1941.
KLEINTJES, P. *Staatsinstellingen van Nederlandsche-Indie*, New York, 1943.
KLOES, W. B. *De toekomstige territoriale begrenzing van Nederland*, Alphen aan den Rijn, 1945.
KNICKERBOCKER WEEKLY, New York, Feb. 27, 1941-
KONINKLIJKE WOORDEN—10 MEI 1940—10 MEI 1941, Batavia, 1941.
KOOP, J. M. *Het arbeidersvraagstuk*, Eindhoven, 1945.
KORS, J. B. *Het vraagstuk eener eigen politieke groepeering van de Nederlandsche Katholieken*, Helmond, 1946.
KORT OVERZICHT VAN FEITEN EN STANDPUNTEN IN NEDERLANDSCH-INDIE, 's—Gravenhage, 1946.
KROESE, A. *The Dutch navy at war*, London, 1945.
——*Neerland's zeemacht in oorlog*, London, 1944.
LANDHEER, B. *Historical background of postwar reconstruction of the Netherlands*, New York, 1942.

——*The legal status of the Netherlands*, New York, 1943.
——ed. *The Netherlands*, Los Angeles, 1943.
——ed. *The Netherlands (condensed)* New York, 1943.
——*The Netherlands East Indies comes of age*, New York, 1942.
——*joint ed. Contribution of Holland to the sciences.* See Barnouw, A.J.
——ed. *Netherlands East Indies.* See U. S. Library of Congress.
——*La nacion holandesa.* Mexico, 1945.
——*Wartime study of Dutch Banking. In Buroughs Clearing House,* 1943.

LANGE, W. DE. *Education and instruction in the Netherlands*, The Hague, 1946.

LASKER, B. *Peoples of Southeast Asia*, New York, 1944.
——*Role of the Chinese in the Netherlands Indies*, New York, 1946.
——*Welfare and freedom in postwar Southeast Asia*, New York, 1942.

LEEUW, A. S. DE. *Nederland in de wereldpolitiek van 1900 tot heden*, Zeist, 1936.

LEHMAN, L. H. *The drama of William of Orange*, New York, 1937.

LICHTVELD, L. *Suriname aan de tweesprong*, Amsterdam, 1945.

LILIENTHAL, P. E. *Asia's captive colonies*, New York, 1944.

LOON, H. W. VAN. *The fall of the Dutch Republic*, Boston, 1924.
——*The golden book of the Dutch navigators*, New York, 1938.
——*The rise of the Dutch Kingdom*, Garden City, 1915.
——*The story of the Pacific*, New York, 1940.

LOS VAN AARLANDERVEEN, V. R. *Het nieuwe ideaal*, Utrecht, 1945.

LOURENS, M. M. *Education in the Netherlands*, New York, 1942.

LUGER, J. *All about Amsterdam*, Amsterdam, 1945.

MANDERE, H. CH. G. J. VAN DER. *Kleine geschiedenis van den grooten oorlog* (1939-1945), Leiden, 1945.

MARSMAN, J. H. *I escaped from Hong Kong*, New York, 1942.

MEIJER RANNEFT, J W. *Rechtvaardigheid voor Indië*, Maastricht, 1945.
——*De weg voor Indie*, Amsterdam, 1945.

MENEFEE, A. G. *The Undigested Indies*, New York, 1944.

MENEFEE, S. C. *Japan's psychological war*, Baltimore, 1943.

MOOK, H. J. VAN, *The Netherlands Indies and Japan*, New York, 1944.
——*Past and future in the Netherlands Indies*, New York, 1945.
——*The position of Europe in Asia*, London, 1942.

MOTLEY, J. L. *History of the United Netherlands,* New York, 1861.
——*The life and death of John of Barneveld,* New York, 1874.
——*The rise of the Dutch republic,* New York, 1875.

MULDER, D. *Uit het leven onzer Koningin,* Paramaribo, 1943.

MULDER, H. A. *Nederland,* Pretoria, 1943.

MURALT, W. J. J. DE. *Nederland heeft een doel,* Maastricht, 1945.

A NATION AT WAR, New York, 1943.

NEDERLANDSCH COMITE VOOR GEBIEDSUITBREIDING. *Is annexatie door Nederland van aangrenzend Duitsch gebied zedelijk verantwoord..* Rotterdam, 1945.

NEDERLANDSCHE MAATSCHAPPIJ VOOR NIJVERHEID EN HANDEL. *Het geldvraagstuk en het schuldenprobleem,* Haarlem, 1945.

NEDERLANDSCHE MAATSCHAPPIJ VOOR NIJVERHEID EN HANDEL. *Sociale organisatie van het bedrijfsleven,* Haarlem, 1945.

NEDERLANDSE VOLKSBEWEGING, AMSTERDAM. *Voor het voetlicht:Schermerhorn en Banning over de N. V. B.,* Amsterdam, 1945.

THE NETHERLANDS BEFORE THE WAR, The Hague, 1945.

THE NETHERLANDS COMMONWEALTH AND THE FUTURE, New York, 1945.

NETHERLANDS NEWS LETTER. New York, Jan. 1946—

NETHERLANDS NEWS (semi-monthly) New York, July 15, 1941—Jan. 1, 1946.

NETHERLANDS NEWS DIGEST (semi-monthly) New York, March 15, 1942—March 1944.

NETHERLANDS ORANGE BOOK. The Hague, Min. of Foreign Affairs, 1940.

NIEUWE HART VAN ROTTERDAM, Rotterdam, 1946.

NIEUWENHUYSEN, W. L. VAN. *De Noordzee-delta,* Deventer, 1945.

NISPEN TOT SEVENAER, C. M. O. VAN. *Geen inpalming wel inlijving van Duitsch gebied?* Zutphen, 1945.

NYSTROM, J. W. *Surinam,* New York, 1942.

OOSTLAND—ONS LAND. Amsterdam, 1945.

ORGANISATIE VAN HET BEDRIJFSLEVEN, 's—Gravenhage, 1945.

OSBORN, F. *The Pacific world,* New York, 1944.

OUR FARMER'S FIGHT FOR THE FUTURE, Amsterdam, 1946.

PANIKKAR, K. M. *The future of South-East Asia,* New York, 1943.

PLAS, C. O. VAN DER. *Nationalism in the Netherlands Indies,* New York, 1942.

——*Recent developments in the Netherlands East Indies*, New York, 1942.

PREGER, W. *Dutch administration in the Netherlands Indies*, Melbourne, 1944.

QUARITCH, WALES, H. G. *Years of blindness*, New York, 1943.

QUARLES VAN UFFORD, W. C. A. *Nederland's koopvaardij in oorlogstijd*, London, 1945.

THE QUEEN LOOKS AT THE FUTURE, New York, 1943.

QUEEN WILHELMINA'S NAVY, London, 1944.

QUISPEL, H. V. *De koninklijke marine schrijft geschiedenis*, Batavia-C., 1941.

——*Nederlandsch Indie in den tweeden wereldoorlog*, London, 1945.

RADIO SPEECHES, HELD BY HER MAJESTY QUEEN WILHELMINA AND PROFESSOR W. SCHERMERHORN, New York, 1945.

RAUWS, J. *The Netherlands Indies*, London, 1935.

RECOVERY OF DUTCH TRADE AND INDUSTRY, The Hague, Min. of Economic Affairs, 1946.

REGEERINGSALMANAK VOOR NEDERLANDSCH-INDIE, 1942 eerste gedeelte, New York, 1943.

RENIER, G. J. *The Dutch nation*, London, 1944.

——*William of Orange*, New York, 1933.

RHIJN, A. A. VAN, ed. *Nieuw Nederland*, New York, 1944.

RIEMENS, H. *The Netherlands*, New York, 1944.

RIES, L. A. *Inlijving van Duitsch grondgebied is noodzakelijk*, Rotterdam, 1945.

RIPLEY, D. *Trail of the money bird*, New York, 1942.

ROBINSON, W. L. *The Netherlands navy fights on*, Annapolis, 1944.

ROMEIN, J. *Nieuw Nederland*, Amsterdam, 1945.

ROYAL INSTITUTE OF INTERNATIONAL AFFAIRS. Netherlands overseas territories, London, 1941.

ROYAL NETHERLANDS INDIES ARMY, NEW YORK. *Het vrouwenkorps van het Koninklijk Nederlandsch-Indisch leger*, New York, 1944.

THE ROYAL NETHERLANDS NAVY, New York, 1944.

RUTTEN, L. M. R. *Science in the Netherlands Indies*, Amsterdam, 1925.

SANDICK, A. A. VAN. *Herstel der maatschappij*, Rotterdam, 1945.

SASSEN, F. *Eenheid en verscheidenheid in het Nederlandsche volk*, Nijmegen, 1945.

SCHAKEL, P. *Wij deelgenooten*, Amsterdam, 1945.

SCHELTEMA, M. W. *Het nieuwe Nederland,* Alphen aan den Rijn, 1945.

SCHORER, G. L. *Annexatie een recht en een plicht,* Amsterdam, 1945.

SCHOUTEN, J. *Partijformatie en partijgroepeering,* Wageningen, 1945.

SCHRIEKE, J. J. *The administrative system of the Netherlands Indies,* New York, 1939.

——*Inleiding in het staatsrecht van Nederlands-Indië,* New York, 1943.

SCHRIEKE, B. *The educational system in the Netherlands Indies,* New York, 1938.

——*The effect of western influence on native civilizations in the Malay Archipelago,* Batavia, 1929.

SHORT ACCOUNT OF MILITARY AND NAVAL OPERATIONS IN THE NEDERLANDS, London, Nederlandsch Dept. van oorlog en marine, 1943.

SIERENBERG DE BOER, G. W. J. VAN. *Sociale en economische ordening,* Alphen aan den Rijn, 1946.

SITSEN, P. H. W. *The industrial development of the Netherlands Indies,* New York, 1942.

SJAHRIR, S. (SJAHRAZAD, *pseud.) Indonesische overpeinzingen,* Amsterdam, 1945.

——*Onze strijd,* Amsterdam, 1946.

SLAMET, M. *Japanese "Dalang" (shadowplayer),* Batavia, 1946.

——*Holy war "made in Japan,"* Batavia, 1946.

——*Aftermath of the Japanese occupation,* Batavia, 1946.

——*Japanese intrigues,* Amsterdam, 1946.

SCHMIDT, P. J. *Buitenlandsche politiek van Nederland,* Leiden, 1945.

SMIT, C. *Buitenlandsche politiek van Nederland,* 's—Gravenhage, 1945.

SNELLER, Z. W. *Geschiedenis van den Nederlandschen landbouw,* 1795-1940, Groningen, 1943.

SOCIALE ZEKERHEID, *rapport v. d. Commissie tot bestudeering der sociale verzekering in Nederland,* London, 1944-1945.

STAATSBLADEN V. H. KONINKRIJK DER NEDERLANDEN, 1940-1945, Zwolle, 1945.

STATISTICAL ABSTRACT OF THE NETHERLANDS EAST INDIES, 1940, New York, 1943.

STIKKER, A. H. *Economie v. d. Indische archipel,* New York, 1943.

SUGGESTIONS PRESENTED BY THE NETHERLANDS GOVERNMENT, CONCERNING THE PROPOSALS FOR THE MAINTENANCE OF PEACE AND SECURITY AGREED ON AT THE FOUR POWER CONFERENCE OF DUMBARTON OAKS, 1945.

SUURHOFF, J. G. *Staking . . . ja of neen?* Amsterdam, 1945.

SWEERS, B. M. *Vrije meeningen in een vrij land,* Amsterdam, 1946.

TAYLOR, H. C. *World trade in agricultural products,* New York, 1943.

TAYLOR, N. *Cinchona in Java,* New York, 1945.

TEN YEARS OF JAPANESE BURROWING IN THE NETHER-
LANDS EAST INDIES, New York, 1942.

TERPSTRA, H. *Buitenlandsche getuigen van onze koloniale expansie,*
Amsterdam, 1944.

THEY HAD 7 MONTHS. The Netherlands Railways, Utrecht, 1946.

THOMPSON, V. *Japan' blueprint for Indonesia,* New York, 1946.
——*Government and nationalism in Southeast Asia, See title entry.*

TINBERGEN, J. *Economische bewegingsleer,* Amsterdam, 1943.
——*International economic co-operation,* New York, 1946.

U. N. R. R. A. WELFARE DIVISION. *The Netherlands,* London,
1944.

U. S. DEPT. OF LABOR. *Labor conditions in the Netherlands,* Washington, 1944.

U. S. DEPT. OF LABOR. *Labor conditions in the Netherlands Indies,*
Washington, 1944.

U. S. LIBRARY OF CONGRESS. *Netherlands East Indies, a bibliography,* Washington, D. C., 1945.

U. S. OFFICE OF WAR INFORMATION. *De strijd in den Grooten
Ocean,* New York, 1945.

U. S. WAR DEPT. *An annotated bibliography of the Southwest Pacific and adjacent areas,* New York, 1944.

U. S. WAR DEPT. *A pocket guide to Netherlands East Indies,* Washington, 1943.

UNIVERSITY OF CHICAGO ROUND TABLE. *Revolt in the South
Pacific,* Chicago, 1944.

VANDENBOSCH, A. *The Dutch East Indies,* Berkeley, 1942.
——*Dutch in the Far East,* New York, 1943.
——*Netherlands Indies,* New York, 1944.

VEN, C. H. W. VAN DER. *Naar ruimer horizon,* Den Helder, 1945.

VERAART, J. A. *Holland,* London, 1944.
——*Inleiding tot de Nederlandsche constitutie,* London, 1945.

VERDOORN, F. *Scientific institutions,* New York, 1945.

VERDOORN, J. A. *Zending en het Indonesisch nationalisme,* Amsterdam, 1945.

VEREENIGING VOOR OPINIE-ONDERZOEK. *Mededeelingenblad,*
's—Gravenhage, 1945—

VERSLAG VAN DE COMMISSIE TOT BESTUDERING VAN STAATSRECHTELIJKE HERVORMINGEN, Batavia, 1941.

VISMAN, F. H. *The provisional government of the Netherlands East Indies*, New York, 1945.

——*Situation in Java*, New York, 1946.

——*Visman rapport*. See *Verslag van de Commissie tot bestudeering van staatsrechtelijke hervormingen*.

VISSER 'T HOOFT, W. A. *The struggle of the Dutch Church*, New York, 1945.

VISSER 'T HOOFT, W. A., comp. *Holländsche kirchendokumente*, Zürich, 1944.

VLEKKE, B. H. M. *Evolution of the Dutch nation*, New York, 1945.

——*The Netherlands and the United States*, Boston, 1945.

——*Nusantara*, Cambridge, 1943.

——*Post-war educational reconstruction in the Netherlands*, New York, 1944.

——*The story of the Dutch East Indies*, Cambridge, 1945.

VOLLENHOVEN, M. W. R. VAN. *Wat nu*, Driebergen, 1945.

VOORTLAND, A. *Indisch getij Hollandsche bakens*, Maastricht, 1944.

VOORTLAND, A. and DE KEIZER, W. G. N. *En nu . . . Indië*, Maastricht, 1944.

VRIJ NEDERLAND (weekly) London, Aug. 3, 1940— (since April 6, 1946 *Stem van Nederland*)

WEISGLAS, M. *Economisch Nederland*, 's—Gravenhage, Min. v. Econ. zaken, 1946.

WENTHOLT, W. *Naar saneering van den gulden*, Amsterdam, 1945.

WERKMAN, E. *Nederland bouwt tunnels*, Amsterdam, 1946.

WERTHEIM, W. F. *Nederland op den tweesprong*, Arnhem, 1946.

WESTERMAN, J. C., ed. *Vreemden over Indië*, 's—Gravenhage, 1946.

WEYER, G. A. P. *Holland and the Netherlands Indies*, New York, 1945.

——*Nederlands taak in Indië*, New York, 1945.

WIJ VAREN WEER, Amsterdam, 1946.

WIDJOJOATMODJO, A. *Islam in the Netherlands East Indies*, New York, 1943.

WILBUR, M. E. *The East India company and the British empire in the Far East*, New York, 1945.

WILSON, H. E. *American education and the Far East*, Washington, 1942.

WINSEMIUS, A. *Opbouw v. h. bestuursapparaat*, Amsterdam, 1945.

WITBOEK BETREFFENDE DE MAATREGELEN TOT ZUIVER-
ING V. H. GELDWEZEN IN NEDERLAND. 's—Gravenhage, 1946.

WITLOX, J. *Onze eigen politieke organisatie blijve*, Bussum, 1945.

WORMSER, C. W. *Indië-vaart*, Leiden, 1946.

WRIGHT, J. K. *The Netherlands West Indies*, New York, 1941.

ZEEGERS, G. H. L. *Een ernstige beslissing*, The Hague, 1945.

ZOETMULDER, S. H. A. M., ed. *Nederland in den oorlog zooals het
werkelijk was*, Utrecht, 1946.